Japan, Korea, and China

Japan, Korea, and China

American Perceptions and Policies

DS
518.8
J 35

William Watts
George R. Packard
Ralph N. Clough
Robert B. Oxnam
Potomac Associates

Lexington Books
D.C. Heath and Company
Lexington, Massachusetts
Toronto

Library of Congress Cataloging in Publication Data

Main entry under title:

Japan, Korea, and China.

    Includes index.
    1. East Asia—Foreign relations—United States. 2. United States—Foreign relations—East Asia. I. Watts, William, 1930-
DS518.8.J35   327.5'073   78-7128
ISBN 0-669-02470-8

Published simultaneously in Canada

Printed in the United States of America

International Standard Book Number: 0-669-02470-8

Library of Congress Catalog Card Number: 78-7128

Contents

Preface

Over the past forty years, the United States has had a bittersweet relationship with Asia. We are heirs to the history of World War II, Korea, and Vietnam, just as we are also heirs to the Occupation of Japan and to the enormous economic growth of many Asian nations in the past quarter century. Those legacies, negative and positive, have prodded us into a new era during the 1970s. So far it is an era of peace among the great powers, an era of détente and exploration of new strategic and economic relationships. But it is also an era of uncertainty with many policy choices lying ahead. We need to think about these alternatives and the complex issues that surround them. And we need to consider these options against the domestic political situation and the mood of the public in the United States.

This volume, the latest in the continuing series of foreign policy studies from Potomac Associates, focuses on one of the most important and at the same time potentially dangerous areas of the world: east and northeast Asia. Within this region, the interests of four of the world's major powers—the United States, Japan, the People's Republic of China, and the Soviet Union—intersect. Two long-standing American allies, the Republic of Korea and the Republic of China on Taiwan, are also involved. Rival claims for power both in China and on the Korean peninsula remain unresolved. The potential for armed hostilities continues, albeit reduced from the maximum tension with the signing of the Korean Armistice and the improvement of relations between Washington and Peking. The emergence of Japan as one of the world's most dynamic and powerful economies, the growing role of the People's Republic of China in the international arena, and the remarkable economic gains of both the Republic of Korea and the Republic of China have altered the structure of virtually every bilateral and multilateral relationship in this critical corner of the globe.

Several fundamental developments have contributed to this process. These include the more limited definition of the role of the United States in Asia by the Nixon administration, the reduced American military presence in Asia following the end of the war in Vietnam, and the dramatic U.S. initiative toward Peking. Our friends and foes alike have been forced to ask themselves some basic questions about the nature and endurance of the U.S. commitment in Asia. At the same time, American relations with the area have never been greater: in 1977, for the first time in history, our trade with Asia exceeded trade with Europe. Crucial long-term policy decisions will be made as each of the parties involved seeks new alternatives and the establishment of new, revised, or reinforced relationships. The challenges to leaders in every capital are large and difficult.

In the pages that follow, we have attempted to do three things. First, we examine the current state of relationships between the United States and the other countries involved—Japan, South Korea, North Korea, the People's Republic of China, and the Republic of China. The nature of our ties, or lack of them, with each country is assessed. We address some of the outstanding differences or problems, each in the framework of developments over the past few years.

Second, we analyze the state of American opinion toward each of the countries, their peoples, some of their policies, and certain alternative policies that the United States might undertake.

Finally, in each case we suggest some new policy directions for the United States, and consider these within the framework of public opinion in this country. While such popular moods do not dictate the course of U.S. policy, they do exert pressures on our leaders, and provide one major element to be reckoned with in the policy-making process.

We do not, of course, pretend to have all the answers. Rather, we hope that our analysis and recommendations will contribute in a useful way to the ongoing debate that surrounds any initiatives that may be taken by the White House, Congress, American business and the private sector, and the corresponding institutions in the other countries concerned.

Japan is the subject of the first chapter. Here, our focus is on the two key areas of economics and security. Japan's relations with China and the Soviet Union are discussed as a backdrop for a closer look at some of the more difficult and controversial problems now on the bilateral agenda between the United States and Japan. These include our mutual security arrangements and the question of a new look at Japan's self-defense role. The troublesome spillover arising from the enormous trade imbalance between our two countries is considered, as are a number of narrower, but nonetheless irksome issues, such as disagreements on civil air routes and Japan's desire to develop plutonium-based energy. We look at the pervasive impact of American culture on post-World War II Japanese society, and the growing desire on the part of the Japanese to play a more independent and prominent role on the world state.

In chapter 2, we turn to the Korean peninsula, and the frustrating efforts to find a more stable relationship between north and south. The nature of U.S. security ties with South Korea is examined in some detail, giving special attention to the planned U.S. troop withdrawals from that country and the south's requirements for future security and self-defense. The impact of "Koreagate" and alleged influence-buying efforts in the U.S. Congress is assessed, particularly in terms of its influence on American perceptions and of outlooks toward South Korea. We also examine the effect of South Korea's impressive economic growth and the effect of its human rights issues on popular attitudes and policy deliberations.

Finally, in chapter 3 we consider the monumental policy shifts that have occurred between the United States and China, and the continuing dilemma of the "normalization" of diplomatic relations that confronts the Carter administration. We examine prospects for changed relations with Taiwan, as well as the growing interaction with the People's Republic of China. We review several "formulas" for sorting out diplomatic, economic, and cultural ties between Washington, Peking, and Taipei. We outline what we see as the legitimate concerns of all three parties, urging a compromise that is acceptable and fair to each.

The survey research that provided the base for our analysis of American attitudes toward these complex and often interrelated questions was carried out in two phases. Polling concerning Japan and Korea was carried out in April 1978, with field work handled by the Gallup Organization. This survey also included a number of other questions dealing with American perceptions of the importance of Europe versus Asia, the relative importance of nations around the world to U.S. interests, support for U.S. troop commitments abroad, and willingness to come to the defense of selected allies in the event of attack. The questions on China were asked in April 1977, with some updating in the 1978 survey. These results have been enhanced by being placed in the context of earlier Potomac Associates' survey research, as well as relevant efforts undertaken by others.

We hope that readers will find our analysis and policy recommendations helpful in clarifying the important but often murky debates that surround the topics we have addressed. We are well aware that others might take different approaches and come to different conclusions, but if our efforts serve to stimulate serious discussion and open the way to fresh alternatives, then we will have more than achieved our goal.

Acknowledgments

The authors wish to acknowledge with deep gratitude the generosity of the following individuals and organizations, whose support and encouragement have made this work possible: T. Jefferson Coolidge, Jr., Arthur M. Dubow, the China Council of The Asia Society, the Corning Glass Works Foundation, the Fluor Corporation, the Ford Foundation, the Japan Society, Inc., the Marine Midland Bank, the Rockefeller Foundation, the Sumitomo Fund for Policy Research Studies, and the Westinghouse Electric Corporation.

In addition, we wish to thank our many colleagues whose advice and counsel contributed so much to our efforts. T. Jefferson Coolidge, Jr. and Arthur M. Dubow provided especially helpful comments and suggestions on many portions of the manuscript, and Dr. Lloyd A. Free and Charles W. Roll, Jr. assisted greatly in the design and interpretation of the survey questions.

Shevaun McDarby and Mary Poggioli did an outstanding job of typing and retyping the manuscript under great time pressures. Jayne Wise handled proofreading with high professional skill.

The contents of the pages that follow are, of course, solely the responsibility of the authors.

Part I:
Japan

1 Policy Setting

In the past half century, the relationship between Japan and the United States has survived wrenching crises: mistrust, rivalry, surprise attack, bloody warfare, occupation, and a long series of painful adjustments toward a restoration of trust. The current 26-year-old alliance between the two former enemies, fashioned during the cold war out of common economic, political, and security interests, is nevertheless as strong and deeply rooted today as any that has ever existed between nations of East and West. Trade between Japan and the United States—$29 billion worth in 1977—is the largest by far that has ever flowed across an ocean between two nations. Japan is America's second largest market; America is the largest buyer of Japanese products. Japan is the only great power outside Western civilization to have adopted the democratic principles and humanistic values cherished by most Americans.

The first non-Western nation to achieve miraculous economic growth, Japan in 1978 was on the brink of surpassing the United States in average per capita income. With its gross national product of more than $800 billion, third highest in the world, Japan is in a position to play a major role in aiding less developed nations. And the Japanese have achieved all this modernization and have accepted Western influences without losing their cultural identity and sense of pride in their special characteristics.

Problems remain on both sides of the Pacific Ocean. Japan still depends on the United States for its security vis-à-vis the Soviet Union and the People's Republic of China. This rankles the Japanese; much of their history in the past several centuries can be seen as a long and anguished quest for self-sufficiency. They have difficulty reconciling their new wealth with their limited role in world politics and with their realization that, now more than ever, they are dependent on other nations for fuel, food, other raw materials, and markets.

Although Japan's economic interests reach every corner of the world, the distinctive Japanese language and culture—which form the very essence of their sense of security and well being—to a large degree keep them isolated from the mainstream of thought and cultural intercourse in the shrinking global community.

The United States, which wholeheartedly supported Japan's economic growth and military dependency after World War II, today finds itself facing huge, unprecedented deficits ($31.1 billion in 1977) in its world trade,

3

with about one-fourth of the deficit ($8 billion) arising from its trade deficit with Japan. Many American industries and workers feel threatened by a flood of Japanese imports. Despite Japanese efforts to curb exports in selected products, American policy makers increasingly feel that Japan should restrain its trade practices even more, open up its own markets more fully, and assume a greater share of the burden for its own defense.

Other complex problems have arisen recently as a result of President Carter's desire to withdraw American ground forces from South Korea and to limit the spread of plutonium technology. Despite the carefully nurtured bonds of friendship and understanding in the diplomatic, business, and academic communities in both countries, there persists in America a tendency to look first toward Europe, to ignore or look down on Asians, and, with what seems to many Japanese to border on racial prejudice, to take the alliance with Japan less seriously than with our more familiar Atlantic allies.

Postwar Japan

To understand the issues facing the United States and Japan today, it is necessary to note briefly the extraordinary events since the explosion of atomic bombs on Hiroshima and Nagasaki in August 1945, the surrender of the Japanese aboard the *U.S.S. Missouri*, and the 6½ years in which Japan, for the first time in its history, was occupied by a foreign power.

Occupation Reforms

Despite the long and bitter war in the Pacific and American fears that the Japanese would fight to the last to defend their home islands, after surrender the Japanese responded with surprising docility and even eagerness to the reforms imposed by General Douglas MacArthur and the American occupation forces. Having experimented with constitutional government in the early part of this century, before military leaders seized power in the 1930s, Japan's highly educated, skilled population responded with enthusiasm to many of the occupation-sponsored reforms: changing the emperor from a divine chief of state to a symbolic figure; abolishing the peerage; dissolving the armed forces; including in their constitution Article IX, which renounced "war as a sovereign right of the nation and the threat of use of force as a means of settling international disputes" and asserted "land, sea, and air forces as well as other war potential will never be maintained"; breaking up the huge cartels (*zaibatsu*); giving peasants their own farms through land reform; encouraging the formation of strong labor

unions and a free press; and establishing a parliamentary democracy model-
ed generally after the British system. To a degree that has surprised even
some authors of the occupation reforms, democracy has taken deep root in
Japan and to this day flourishes in a unique combination of Western
parliamentary politics and traditional Japanese arrangements of power.

Diplomatic Recovery

Beginning with independence in 1952 and continuing for the next 20 years,
the two main priorities for successive Japanese governments were to recover
from the losses of World War II through diplomacy and to rebuild the nation's economic strength—in each case, mainly through close relations with
the United States. Japanese prime ministers and diplomats worked
singlemindedly and with great success to achieve these aims.

Japan's independence was restored in 1952 when American forces were
fighting North Korea and mainland China on the Korean peninsula.
Therefore Washington sought in the peace and security treaties of 1952 to
build up Japan as rapidly as possible as a counter to the rapidly rising communist power in Asia. To ensure that Japan would be a stable, prospering
democracy, Washington helped Japan regain access to world markets and
raw materials. On the military side, Washington changed abruptly from its
policy of demilitarizing Japan to encouraging the Japanese to rearm even
faster than most Japanese wished to move. By 1954 Japan had begun to
develop its own self-defense forces, which today number 238,000.

By the late 1950s, the security treaty, which permitted the United States
to station 100,000 troops at some 1400 bases and facilities throughout
Japan and use them for its own purposes throughout Asia, was seen by
many Japanese as an undesirable extension of the occupation—a price
Japan had to pay to achieve freedom, an affront to its reviving national
pride, and possibly even a lightning rod that could draw the country into
another war. A new security treaty was signed in 1960, removing the more
objectionable provisions and giving Japan a greater voice, through prior
consultation, in changes in the equipment, deployment, and combat operations of American forces based in Japan. Opposition to even this new treaty
by left wing parties, unions, and students led to a prolonged and massive
protest movement in Tokyo. It was climaxed by street violence, the
cancellation of President Eisenhower's planned visit in June 1960, and the
resignation of Prime Minister Kishi, who was seen as high-handed and
subservient to Washington, even by members of his own party. But the
furor soon subsided, and the treaty remains in force today, even though
either country may abrogate it at any time by giving one year's notice of intent.

Controversy over the treaty has all but subsided in recent years and is likely to arise again only if hostilities break out in or near Japan. Most Japanese have come to accept the treaty as a necessary, if sometimes irritating, fact of life in a potentially hostile world. The current treaty commits each party to join in resisting "armed attack against either party in the territories under the administration of Japan," but does not commit Japan to help the United States resist attacks elsewhere. The United States is committed today, through this treaty and through other statements and agreements, to use its nuclear umbrella to defend Japan from external attack. Japan has insisted, however, that U. S. nuclear weapons not be stationed on its soil; nor will the United States store, manufacture, or introduce nuclear weapons into Japan.

Aside from winning these changes in the security treaty, Japanese diplomats worked steadily to eliminate the remaining vestiges of defeat. In 1956 Japan signed a declaration ending the state of war with the Soviet Union and reopening relations with Moscow. The next year it began to loosen trade restrictions with the People's Republic of China. In 1956 it joined the United Nations; and in 1958, with United States' support, it was elected to a seat on the UN Security Council. In 1965 Japan normalized relations with South Korea. In 1966 it won from the United States the return of the Bonin Islands and an agreement to negotiate the return of Okinawa. Finally, in 1972, after long negotiations, Okinawa reverted to Japanese sovereignty, and Japan normalized relations with the People's Republic of China. With the exception of a formal peace treaty with the Soviet Union—still held up by Soviet refusal to return to Japan four small islands at the southern tip of the Kurile chain off Hokkaido—the era of postwar diplomacy had ended successfully for Japan just 20 years after the end of the U. S. occupation. A new era of more complex choices began.

Economic Regeneration

On the economic front, recovery was even more spectacular. Japan is faced today with the problems of startling success. A small, resource-poor island country with 114 million people in an area about the size of Montana, with only about 17 percent arable land, Japan has of necessity become mainly an importer of raw materials and an exporter of manufactured goods. After World War II, the Japanese government undertook a program of rapid growth with concentration on building up the private sector, through conservative fiscal policies, cheap bank financing, high savings and investment rates, wholesale and export price stability, and careful identification and exploitation of foreign markets. Government and business leaders closely cooperated in these policies, and organized labor generally supported them.

Thus, Japanese industry concentrated on increasing productivity, expanding domestic and foreign markets, and making its prices competitive. An advantage peculiar to Japan was the protection afforded by the security treaty with the United States, which allowed Japan to devote less than 1 percent of GNP to defense each year.

From 1949 to 1973, Japan's real GNP grew at an average annual compound rate of 9.5 percent. In the same period, real exports rose 14.7 percent annually, and real per capita income increased 8.3 percent per year. In the two decades after regaining independence, the Japanese raised their real income from the level of poverty to affluence.

During this period, Japanese industry gradually moved away from the labor-intensive manufacture of textiles, apparel, and handicrafts toward capital-intensive and higher-technology production such as steel, automobiles, ships, machinery, electronics, chemicals, and nonferrous metals. Japan's concentration on exports in these basic industries led to pressure for protectionist policies in other countries which could not compete with Japanese prices and quality and which suffered high rates of unemployment in these industries as a result.

Protectionist sentiment sprang up in the United States in some of the sectors affected by these products. From 1952 to 1965 there had been, of course, sporadic squabbles between the two countries over specific Japanese exports—flatware and cotton blouses, for example. But the United States had taken a generally benign view of Japan's rapid export expansion, on the premise that a healthy Japan depended on economic growth, which in turn depended on exporting enough goods to pay for imports of food and industrial raw materials. On the same premise, the United States had strongly backed Japan's entry into the General Agreement on Tariffs and Trade (GATT) and tolerated Japanese protection of its own industry through quotas and other trade restrictions.

By 1965, however, Japan had become a nation with a balance-of-payments surplus—a net exporter to the world—and by 1969 its chronic deficit vis-à-vis the United States had shifted to a chronic surplus. The potential for confrontation grew larger when in 1972 the United States ran a huge international trade deficit—$6.4 billion. The textile controversy of 1969-1971 was a harbinger of serious and continuing trade disputes.

The textile controversy, ironically, involved basically weak and declining industries in each country; but since it touched raw political nerves in Washington and Tokyo, it grew to rancorous proportions. Claiming that imports of Japanese synthetic and woolen textile products were injuring their sales and threatening jobs, American textile interests, in return for election support, prevailed on President Nixon to press for tight controls on Japanese exports of these products. Nixon thought he had made a deal with Prime Minister Sato in late 1969; for the return of a "nuclear-free"

Okinawa to Japan, Sato would undertake to persuade Japan's textile industry to restrict voluntarily exports to the United States. In the end, however, Sato was unable (or unwilling) to deliver on this bargain, and tension rose. Nixon asked Congress to enact quotas on these products, but the bill died. Japanese textile leaders then angered Nixon by striking a deal for milder, voluntary quotas with Congressman Wilbur Mills, then powerful chairman of the House Ways and Means Committee, a deal which Nixon promptly denounced. For the first time since the end of the war, responsible voices in Washington questioned whether support for "Japan Inc." was in the American interest. The dispute was finally resolved in the wake of the "Nixon shocks" (discussed below) when the United States threatened to impose textile quotas by Executive order under the Trading with the Enemy Act if an agreement was not reached by October 15, 1971. The Japanese yielded and signed an agreement limiting exports.

End of the Honeymoon

The end of the long "honeymoon" in United States-Japanese relations came in the summer of 1971 with the "Nixon shocks." The July 15 announcement of President Nixon's intention to visit the People's Republic of China stunned the Japanese. For two decades American leaders had been urging the Japanese government to assist in containing "Communist China" and promising that they would inform and consult Tokyo in advance with respect to China policy. In diplomatic circles, "Asakai's nightmare" was the jocular reference in the 1960s to the fears of the then Japanese Ambassador in Washington, Koichiro Asakai, that the Americans would make such a move toward Peking without telling him in advance. It could not happen, the State Department had promised. And then, in 1971, it did.

Hard on the heels of this shock to the Japanese came another: on August 15, Nixon announced a temporary freeze on wages and prices, a temporary 10 percent surcharge on imports, and a floating of the dollar aimed at changing international exchange rates and especially at appreciating the *yen*, again without prior warning to the Japanese.

These shocks came against a background of growing disenchantment with the belief among the Japanese that the United States was omnipotent—a myth fostered by General MacArthur and widely accepted by many Japanese, for whom the American presence was an overwhelming force. Most Japanese came to see American involvement in Vietnam, for instance, as a foolish, wasteful venture, unworthy of a great power. The bombing of North Vietnam was seen by many as evidence of American indifference to the value of Asian lives and ignorance of Asian nationalism.

Twenty years after independence, Japan lived in a different world, with new opportunities and new dangers. On one hand, the threat of communism seemed to have subsided; the Russians and Chinese, instead of uniting to expand communist power in Asia, were snarling at each other. On the other hand, the Organization of Petroleum-Exporting Countries (OPEC), in the wake of the 1973 Yom Kippur war, quadrupled the price of oil, the lifeblood of Japan's economy. Japan must import 99 percent of its oil, three-quarters of it from the Middle East. A serious case of jitters replaced the confident Japanese mood of the early 1970s. A severe round of inflation, followed by a recession from 1974 to 1977, dampened hopes of sustaining the miraculous growth rate of the previous decade.

Meanwhile, Japan's American ally seemed less and less reliable in this new multipolar world. In 1973, a brief United States embargo on the export of soybeans made leaders in Tokyo wonder about dependence on the United States as a source of supply of a key food product to the Japanese. The Watergate scandal seemed to paralyze Washington for two years, and it was followed in Tokyo by a bribery scandal involving the Lockheed Corporation, which forced Prime Minister Kakuei Tanaka out of office.

These jolts brought mixed results. On one hand, Japanese began for the first time since World War II to see Americans realistically, as fallible human beings, rather than as omnipotent defenders of their interest. On the other hand, some of the trust built up over two decades began to erode, and thoughtful Japanese raised questions about the wisdom of relying too much on close ties with the United States.

Outwardly, at least, the two nations continued to maintain warm diplomatic relations. In 1974, Gerald Ford made his first overseas trip to Japan as President, and in 1975, for the first time in history, the Emperor of Japan visited Washington. Public opinion polls still showed that the Japanese felt generally friendly toward the United States and supported the security treaty. Japanese traveled in ever larger numbers to our shores. The strong friendship clearly survived but was overlaid with nervousness. Japan continued to explore ways to diversify its sources of raw materials and markets and to reduce the risks it perceived in its alliance with the United States. It was clear by 1978 that serious economic and political problems remained to be solved and that a dangerous new period of uncertainty lay ahead.

Domestic Politics in Japan

Before these problems are discussed, a few comments on the domestic political scene in Japan since World War II may prove useful. Postwar politics has been dominated by cautious, pragmatic, conservative, and like-minded leaders who have placed economic recovery and rapid growth at the top of the national agenda. Beginning with Shigeru Yoshida, who emerged as the strongest political figure at the end of the occupation, and continuing through Prime Ministers Hatoyama, Kishi, Ikeda, Sata, Tanaka, Miki, and Fukuda, these extraordinary politicians have, with only minor variations in emphasis, formed coalitions within the Diet and among top bureaucrats, banking, and business interests to steer the economy toward high growth and broadly distributed wealth within a framework of considerable freedom for the private sector and relatively low taxation. (Since 1952, overall corporate and personal tax incidence in Japan has been at a rate of approximately 20 percent, compared with roughly 30 percent in the United States.) The cornerstone of their foreign policy has been the alliance with the United States and the close economic relations that have flowed from it.

The Japanese voters have responded to the nearly miraculous success of these policies by returning the Liberal Democratic Party (LDP) to power in all general elections since the party was formed in 1955. Vigorous challenges from the opposition Marxists (the Socialist and Communist parties), as well as the Democratic Socialist and Clean Government (Komeito) parties, have failed to break the LDP's grip on power.

Because of the increase in Japan's urban population and the gradual decline in their rural power base, however, the Liberal Democrats have been winning smaller and smaller proportions of the popular vote. After securing a clear majority of 57.8 percent in 1958, the party entered into a long period of continual decline to 48.8 percent in 1967, 47.9 percent in 1972, and 41.8 percent in 1976. Even with less than a majority of the popular vote, however, the LDP has managed to retain a majority of Diet seats by joining forces with independent members. Given the continuing erosion of the party's agrarian base, however, many observers wonder how much longer the LDP can hold the reins of government. There has been a good deal of speculation about what new forces may emerge to take power in Japan should the LDP lose its grasp.

The best estimates are that the party's decline may be bottoming out; that none of the opposition parties has now, or is likely to have in the foreseeable future, the ability to gain a majority of Diet seats; and that the LDP will remain in power, either by virtue of its own popularity or by forging alliances with centrist elements in some of the other parties. Only a major domestic or international crisis is thought capable of dimming the party's future.

Nevertheless, the declining support for the LDP and the growing strength of the combined opposition have already affected both domestic and foreign policies. The government has been rendered even more cautious, more susceptible to lengthy internal debate aimed at achieving compromise and consensus, and even less prone to take bold, high-risk steps. In fact, one of the remarkable facts about the current political scene in Japan is the great degree of consensus that has been reached on both foreign and domestic issues. The LDP has been pushed toward more government participation in welfare and public works projects by the leftist opposition, and the leftists, despite their continuing lip service to Marxism, have moved toward the center of the political spectrum. Even the rigidly Marxist Socialist party, for example, now supports maintenance of the self-defense forces at about their present level, whereas in the 1950s and 1960s they were totally and sometimes violently opposed to the self-defense forces. The public supports the American-written Constitution so strongly that conservative politicians seldom talk about revising the "no-war" Article IX and other "liberal" aspects of the document. A 1977 poll taken by the Defense Agency indicated that 83 percent of the Japanese people support the maintenance of the self-defense forces at their present strength.

Foreign policy issues scarcely enter into the arena of political controversy. All parties agree that greater independence in foreign affairs would be desirable, but no leader or party has come up with a plausible alternative to the alliance with the United States. While there is much soul searching among intellectuals and in the mass media for a new, more assertive, more distinctive international role for Japan, there is little inclination to take risks or to place Japan's prestige on the line for the sake of new policies. Contributing to the government's caution in foreign affairs are the strong and entrenched bureaucracies at the Ministry of International Trade and Industry, the Finance Ministry, and other key ministries whose support must be enlisted for new policy initiatives. These bureaucrats are inherently cautious in outlook and lean toward the status quo.

The modest international initiatives the Japanese have taken, such as seeking a place as a permanent member of the UN Security Council or establishing a United Nations University in Tokyo, have met with little enthusiasm in international forums and doubtless have discouraged the Japanese from more ambitious enterprises. The widely shared feeling among both the Japanese public and leading politicians is that the nation is at the mercy of international forces beyond its control and that the best policy is prudent survival and continued economic growth. Reaction to foreign events, rather than attempts to manage them, is a deeply rooted behavior pattern in postwar Japan.

It must be added that this assessment is based on the premise that there will be no major upheavals in the current world order: no large-scale wars or worldwide depressions, and uninterrupted access for Japan to overseas markets and sources of raw materials. Major changes on the international scene, however, could lead to major political changes in Japan. Some observers believe that the Japanese could be attracted by a de Gaulle-like figure who issued an emotional call for a Japanese destiny of greater independence and power in the world, playing to the citizen's innate pride and sensitivity to foreign encroachment. This seems an unlikely development, however. Powerful individual leaders have rarely emerged in Japanese history, and demagogues on white chargers stand a better chance in Western nations than in Japan, where self-effacing collective decision making is highly honored. Decisions are thought to arise from consensus within the larger group, and personal ambition is disdained as unacceptable egotism. When strong leadership is exercised in Japan, it is done behind the scenes, shrouded by outer layers of apparent power.

Should foreign upheavals cause the Japanese to feel threatened to the point of requiring decisive government action, the main political thrust likely will come from the right rather than the Marxist left. It will have elements of Pan Asian nationalism; it will lean more toward China than toward Russia; it will have strong anti-Western overtones; and it will seek a new zone of self-sufficiency in Asia and the Pacific. It will find a readiness among Japanese to make sacrifices for clear national purposes. The ultranationalism of the 1930s is not likely to reappear, but the appeal of simple, well-articulated goals remains; and the capacity of the Japanese nation to mobilize to carry out shared objectives remains unsurpassed throughout the world. As evidence, one might point to the great success of their voluntary population control program. Once adopted by Japanese leaders, the nation accepted and stabilized population growth almost overnight.

Japan's Diplomacy in the Far East

Japan's critical need to maintain access to sources of food and raw materials and to overseas markets, coupled with the domestic political constraints discussed above, permits the shape of its diplomacy in the foreseeable future to be predicted with some degree of assurance, once again assuming a stable international setting.

Close military and economic ties with the United States will remain pillars of Japan's foreign policy, despite the current economic strains and several other potentially damaging issues (to be discussed later). Japanese leaders will continue to scrutinize the reliability of their American ally as a supplier of raw materials and as a security partner, but in the absence of a major upheaval the deeply rooted bonds of friendship promise to hold fast.

Japan can be expected, however, to take other steps outside the framework of this alliance to pursue its fundamental aims of reducing world tensions, maintaining freedom of the seas, diversifying its sources of raw materials and its markets, and avoiding dependence on any single foreign country as much as possible. In light of the world's diminishing supply of fossil fuels, Japan's first requirement is to find alternative sources of energy. Japan's thrust into Southeast Asia in the 1930s was motivated by the need to find new sources of oil, and this need has become even more urgent today. As a result, Japan has been pursuing active negotiations with the People's Republic of China, and in early 1978 Japan signed a five-year $20 billion trade agreement which will bring Chinese oil and coal to Japan in exchange for steel and modern plants, equipment, and industrial technology. Japan can be expected to continue to search elsewhere for additional fuel supplies, for instance, in the Soviet Union, via Siberian pipelines, in the seas off Korea, the continental shelf to the south, and in Indonesia.

Toward the Soviet Union and China

Current Japanese policy calls for "equidistance" from the Soviet Union and the People's Republic of China, which means not taking sides in the Sino-Soviet dispute while maximizing trade with each country. The Sino-Soviet dispute offers unique opportunities for adroit Japanese diplomacy; Japan stands to gain as each side seeks Japanese support for its positions.

The Japanese have one important territorial dispute to resolve with the Soviet Union: the four islands at the southern tip of the Kurile chain (Etorofu, Shikotan, Kunashiri, and Habomai) which lie just north of Hokkaido. The Soviet Union seized the islands during World War II and claims them for its own. It has built an airstrip and installed military equipment, and its navy menaces Japanese fishermen in the area. Japan, supported by the United States, insists the islands are and always have been Japanese territory. The issue arises more from Japanese national pride than from any intrinsic value the islands may have; there are virtually no population, resources, or other economic benefits at stake. The Soviet Union has adamantly rejected Japan's claims, possibly because to make any concessions might give added weight to claims against territory seized by the Russians in Eastern Europe during World War II. The dispute has held up conclusion of a final peace treaty between Japan and the Soviet Union, but the two nations have full diplomatic relations based on the 1956 treaty which ended the state of war between them, and their trade (amounting to $3.3 billion in 1977) and other exchanges continue to grow.

Japan and the People's Republic of China finally concluded in 1978 a Treaty of Peace and Friendship, whose purpose was to resolve all the issues remaining from World War II. The major issue was settled in 1972 when Japan withdrew its recognition of the nationalist government of the Republic of China on Taiwan and opened relations with the People's Republic, exchanging ambassadors the following year. Taiwan, which had threatened to sever diplomatic relations with Japan if it recognized the People's Republic, has accepted a new situation in which Japan and Taiwan have exchanged "unofficial" missions and engage in lively trade ($5.2 billion in 1977), far more than Japan's trade with mainland China ($3.4 billion in 1977). Japan thus shares an interest with the United States in seeing that Taiwan's independence is protected from a forcible takeover by the mainland.

One territorial matter remains at issue between Japan and China. The Senkaku Islands (or, as the Chinese call them, Tiao Yu Tai Islands), at the southern tip of the Ryukyu chain below Okinawa, are claimed by both nations. Periodically each exerts its claim of sovereignty by a display of force in the area. The People's Republic insists that the islands are part of Taiwan, which in turn belongs to mainland China, and that they, along with Taiwan, were seized by the Japanese in the Sino-Japanese war of 1894-1895. Japan insists that it laid claim to the islands several years before that war and that they have appeared for many years on international maps as part of Japanese territory. The islands are uninhabited and without important resources. Their value appears to lie in their effect on future claims to rights to mine the seas off mainland China. It seems most unlikely at this time that either China or Japan will permit this dispute to rise to the level of overt hostilities.

The Japanese are drawn by their cultural heritage, written language, and racial origins far more strongly to China than to the Soviet Union, which for many years has been disliked. Many Japanese still remember what seemed to be the traitorous Soviet act in denouncing its neutrality treaty with Japan and joining the allied effort against their country in the closing days of World War II. Thus, if the Chinese continue to be skillful in their diplomacy and deliver on trade agreements, relations between Japan and the People's Republic should improve steadily, despite Japan's formal protestations of "equidistance" from the two communist powers. Japan was willing to risk Soviet anger in 1978 when it signed the peace treaty with the People's Republic, and China is clearly more favored than the USSR in Japan's current mood and diplomacy. The two nation's entirely different economic and political systems and goals will cause problems, but the Chinese surely realize that Japan can be instrumental in assisting the People's Republic to modernize and industrialize and help it take part in cultural and popular exchanges which will facilitate China's reentry into the international order.

Americans can view closer Japan-China relations without nervousness; each side is too committed to its own economic and political system and too nationalistic to join forces against the rest of the world; there is no need to worry about an East Asian "yellow peril."

Toward Southeast Asia

The most striking aspect of Japan's current diplomacy is its renewed interest in Southeast Asia as a trading partner, a source of raw materials, and an arena for political influence. The Japanese long resisted designating Southeast Asia as a special sphere of interest, to avoid arousing wartime memories and on the grounds that Japan now had to act as a "global nation," not an Asian nation, if it were to satisfy its enormous need for markets and raw materials. Until the end of the Vietnam war in 1975, the Japanese claimed they were scrupulously separating politics and economics and that their only interests in Southeast Asia were economic.

Meanwhile Japanese trade, investment, and government aid (usually in the form of loans tied to the purchase of Japanese commodities) have grown by leaps and bounds. Today Southeast Asia is the largest recipient of Japanese private investment among all the developing areas. The region currently receives far more official aid from Japan than it does from the United States. The five members of the Association of Southeast Asian Nations—the Philippines, Malaysia, Singapore, Thailand, and Indonesia—in 1976 received 48 percent of all Japan's "official development assistance" and nearly 12 percent of all Japan's foreign trade ($14 billion). In 1977 Prime Minister Fukuda made an historic trip to Southeast Asia and announced a program of $1 billion in loans in support of regional projects in the ASEAN nations. "The Fukuda doctrine," as this demarche has come to be called, amounts to tacit recognition that Japan does, indeed, have special political interests in Southeast Asia relating to its own economic security, i.e., its need for oil, tin, rubber, and other raw materials and markets of the area, and even "special responsibility," as some Japanese writers have asserted. Among the Japanese there is broad public acceptance of this new, or newly admitted, role. Given the potential of this rapidly developing, relatively peaceful part of the world, Japan's role there is likely to add to its international influence.

All this raises some questions for American diplomacy. Regional groupings such as ASEAN have long been favored in Washington, and Japanese investment in and aid to the developing nations also have been a strongly supported goal. Problems could arise, however, if, on one hand, American businesses find it increasingly difficult to compete in the area where highly skilled Japanese traders have established firm footholds and, on the other hand, Japan continues to rely on the United States Seventh Fleet, the U.S. bases at Subic Bay in the Philippines, and other American military units to maintain peace and stability throughout Southeast Asia. It is not hard to foresee Congress raising questions about the enormous cost of providing military security to the area if the major beneficiaries are to be Japanese corporate interests.

An additional question is whether the Southeast Asian nations themselves will welcome Japanese economic predominance in the region, since in some nations a residue of mistrust lingers from World War II.

Finally, the apparently rising influence of the Soviet Union in Vietnam as well as the strengthened Soviet naval presence in Southeast Asian waters, where China's historic interests cast a long shadow, could lead to increased competition for influence between the two communist powers. The fighting in 1978 between Cambodia, supported by Peking, and Vietnam, supported by the Soviet Union, could be a harbinger of further turmoil.

In any case, Southeast Asia, with its dynamic population, rapid growth rates, rich resources, and strategic position athwart Japan's shipping routes to the Mideast, promises to be the center of attention of Japanese diplomacy in the next decade and an area for either collaboration or competition, or perhaps some of both, between Japan and the United States.

Japan's Relations with the United States

The 1970s brought a new assortment of problems to the American-Japanese alliance. In the two decades following the peace treaty of 1952, the problems were largely bilateral and manageable through prudent government-to-government negotiations. Military and security problems dominated the dialogue, as the United States tried to impose on Japan a supporting role in the Pacific and Japan tried to minimize its risks and burdens and avoid being dragged into American military ventures. Revision of the security treaty in 1960, whereby the number of U. S. installations and troops in Japan was reduced; the return of the Bonin islands (1967) and Okinawa (1972) to Japan; and the prohibition of nuclear weapons at U.S. bases in Japan went far to eliminate the major sources of unhappiness with the security treaty among the Japanese public. But serious questions, mostly in the economic area, remained to be settled.

The Security Treaty

Japanese and Americans have very different perceptions of the American bases and troops stationed on their soil—their purposes, costs, and benefits. Americans, to the extent they are aware of our treaty commitments to Japan at all, tend to see the stationing of troops there as a burden on American taxpayers, but one which is beneficial to both countries in roughly equal measure. Americans, however, need to remember that until

1945 no foreign troops had ever occupied the Japanese islands. The closest threat to Japan came in 1281 when the Kamikaze ("divine wind," or great typhoon) turned back a Mongolian attempt at invasion.

Thus, it was inevitable that a large body of foreign troops, however well disposed they might be, would cause friction between the two nations. And the U. S. military presence, despite the withdrawal of U. S. ground combat troops from the four main islands of Japan, is still a formidable presence. To American military planners, this force is the minimum needed to support the possibility of far-flung operations in the western Pacific from Korea southward to Taiwan, the Philippines, and beyond. To the Japanese public, the perspective is very different.

There are today, if Okinawa is included, 47,000 United States military personnel stationed at 132 different installations throughout Japan. The facilities consist mainly of logistical depots, communication sites, naval bases, airfields for naval and air force units, and hospitals. They include eight major bases, five of them in the crowded Kanto Plains area around Tokyo. There are two important naval bases, Yokosuka and Sasebo, serving the Seventh Fleet. Yokosuka, which can accommodate the largest American aircraft carriers, is the finest naval base in the Pacific next to Pearl Harbor. Except for Marine units based on Okinawa, the United States does not maintain combat troops in Japan.

Okinawa is crucial to the American ability to react with dispatch militarily in the western Pacific, since it is less than 1000 miles from Korea, Taiwan, the Philippines, and mainland China. It is an excellent staging area and operational base, as was demonstrated during the war in Vietnam. B-52's can launch raids from Okinawa and can be refueled over the Kadena Air Force Base in Okinawa. In addition, Naha, the capital of Okinawa, offers good port facilities. Not only is Okinawa the hub of the American communication and air-sea transportation network; but as a logistical base the island also can support a 500,000-man force deployed in the western Pacific. Without Okinawa, the American military deterrent in the Far East would be of questionable credibility.

The Japanese have had a difficult time reconciling the ubiquitous presence of these American forces with their traditional desire for independence and their nationalistic pride. Article IX of the Japanese Constitution prohibits the maintenance of a large military establishment. Since the overwhelming majority of Japanese do not wish to change Article IX, since their own self-defense forces are about as large as they can be without violating Article IX, and since a growing sense of realism about the need for some kind of defense is gradually replacing the almost romantic pacifism or neutralism of the postwar era, the security treaty seems to most Japanese necessary for the foreseeable future. But this does not make American troops and bases particularly palatable, even to those who are strong supporters of the American alliance. The GIs are reminders of the occupation, occupiers of precious land, whites and blacks from an alien culture who deal clumsily with traditional Japanese values and sensibilities. Accidents happen. American jets crash near air bases, killing Japanese citizens. American servicemen commit crimes. The "military culture" of drugs, guns, and tawdry entertainment coexists uneasily in these rigidly civilized environs. The language barrier remains almost insurmountable. Americans need only to imagine a situation in which the Japanese army occupied United States soil to begin to understand Japanese grievances.

As long as the United States' troops and bases are not involved in combat operations and represent no overt threat, most Japanese have come to tolerate them for the time being. Indeed, a recent public opinion survey shows that some 65 percent of the Japanese people support the security treaty. The opposition political parties, which in the 1960s demanded abrogation of the treaty and expulsion of U.S. troops and dismantlement of U.S. bases, now tend to give low priority to these demands in their election rhetoric.

The Thrust of Events

If the current balance of power in East Asia remains roughly as it is today, if there is no war in Korea, and if the U.S. troops and bases are not used to support combat operations elsewhere in Asia, then the Japanese are likely to support the security treaty for the foreseeable future. But three eventualities could change all this.

A Military Threat to Japan. The first eventuality would be the expansion of either Soviet or Chinese power until it appeared to overshadow American military power in the area and to threaten Japan. If, for example, the Soviet Union were perceived in Tokyo as having the ability to gain control of the air and sea around Japan and to cut off Japan's supplies of fuel and raw materials, or the ability to launch a successful communist takeover of the Korean peninsula, or the ability to invade Japan's northern island, Hokkaido, then the security treaty could be seen more as a liability than as a safeguard, more of a provocation against communist neighbors than a guarantee of security. And powerful forces would call for its abrogation.

Even today, some influential Japanese do not believe that the United States would risk a nuclear war with the Soviet Union in order to live up to its treaty commitment to "act to meet the common danger in accordance with its constitutional provisions and processes" in the event of "an armed attack against either Party in the territories under the administration of Japan. . . ." Events since the American defeat in Vietnam have strengthened their doubts: these include the withdrawal of American troops from Thailand, the reduced American military presence in Taiwan, and plans for the withdrawal of U.S. ground forces from South Korea. Doubters argue that Washington gives much attention to the problems of NATO and little attention to Asia in general and to its Japanese ally in particular.

The belief is growing in Japan, moreover, that the United States has fallen behind the Soviet Union in strategic power. A 1977 White Paper on Defense published by Japan's Defense Agency states this belief quite clearly:

> Since the nuclear capabilities of the Soviet Union are numerically superior to those of the United States and since the Soviet Union is improving the quality of its nuclear arsenal at a rapid tempo, the United States is faced with an urgent task to modernize . . . The U.S.S.R. has greatly strengthened its military posture in Europe and the Far East; and as a result some changes are occurring in the military balance between the United States and the Soviet Union and in its structure.[1]

If this perception that the United States lacks either the ability or the will to deter Soviet expansion in East Asia grows, as it appears to be growing now, particularly among Japanese defense planners, new pressures can be expected to arise in Japan against continuation of the security treaty.

Hostilities Involving U.S. Forces Based in Japan. A second scenario that could cause serious problems would be an outbreak of hostilities either on the Korean Peninsula or around the Straits of Taiwan in which U.S. forces based in Japan might become involved.

President Carter's 1977 announcement that the 31,000 U.S. ground combat troops in South Korea would be withdrawn has created some second thoughts in Japan. Even some of the loudest of the critics of the treaty are now finding discomfort in the planned American withdrawal, since Japan could be forced to play a larger role on the Korean Peninsula in the absence of a credible American fighting force there. Since the Korean war broke out in 1950, when Japan was occupied and able to remain aloof from the fighting, most Japanese have tended to view Korea as an "American problem," a game in which they could sit on the sidelines. But the prospect of a greatly reduced U.S. presence in South Korea, the large and growing Japanese trade with South Korea and investment in its dynamic economy, and the presence in Japan of more than 600,000 Korean expatriates of sharply divided loyalties all make it impossible for Tokyo to ignore the Korean problem. For the first time since World War II, Japanese strategic thinkers are facing the implications of an outbreak of hostilities in Korea and the question of how Japan should react to such an event.

In the past two years, the Japanese government has been urging the Carter administration to move slowly on withdrawal and to consult Tokyo at every step along the way while Japanese policy makers consider alternative strategies. There is a general consensus that Japan cannot, under Article IX of the Japanese Constitution, send its self-defense forces into combat overseas. The arguments in favor of keeping U.S. troops in Korea—to deter North Korea from repeating its aggression against the South because of the certainty that American troops would become involved—have been heard with increasing frequency in Japan. The Carter administration has responded by agreeing to phase American troops out of Korea over a five-year period through 1982, and to build up South Korean forces.

To date, the Japanese have not been able to agree on any alternative to the status quo; a large American military presence in both Korea and Japan appears the least undesirable of all the options. Still, the fact that Japan's security is closely tied to that of the Republic of Korea will continue to vex the Japanese, and the economic possibilities will intrigue them. In 1978 the Japanese were willing to face the anger of the People's Republic of China when they signed an agreement with South Korea for joint development of oil resources in a continental shelf area also claimed by the Chinese.

The United States has the right under the security treaty to maintain bases and other facilities in Japan not only for the defense of Japan but also for the maintenance of international peace and security in the Far East. An exchange of notes appended to the 1960 treaty commits the United States to consult with the government of Japan before using facilities in Japan as bases for combat operations, or before making major changes in the deployment in Japan of U.S. armed forces or major changes in their equipment. But this provision has never been invoked—not even during the war in Vietnam, when bases in Japan and Okinawa were of major importance to the American war effort. There is substantial disagreement over what might happen if Japan were to attempt to veto American military plans during prior consultations. Successive Japanese political leaders have argued that they would indeed have a veto power, but the American side has never yielded the point, and it remains to be tested.

In any event, the outbreak of armed combat in Korea would likely lead to a broad public outcry in Japan against any kind of Japanese involvement on the grounds that Japan might be dragged against its will into war. The use of U.S. bases in Japan to support combat operations in Korea could ignite an enormous protest movement against the treaty, a movement which could jeopardize the security and utility of the bases to the U.S. military effort. The Japanese also fear that warfare on the peninsula would send Korean refugees flooding to their shores, creating social turmoil. In short, the current popular acceptance of the security treaty cannot be interpreted as approval of a future combat role for U.S. forces; rather, it reflects a public belief that no outbreak of hostilities is in sight and that the bases are therefore relatively harmless and risk-free.

Waning of Tension. The third scenario which might change the current calculations would be an opposite situation, in which tension might ease so much in East Asia that the U.S. troops and bases might be seen as superfluous. Evidence of this possibility surfaced at the time of the sudden rapprochement between the United States and the People's Republic of China in 1971-1972. Opponents of the treaty who had argued that it entailed high risks for Japan suddenly began to argue that the treaty was no longer necessary since the United States and its adversary were now at peace.

A variation of this argument is that the United States and mainland China are engaged in a game of power politics aimed at stemming the tide of Soviet power in Asia and that Japan is generally irrelevant to the *realpolitik* of the nuclear powers of the region. According to this reasoning, the United States cannot be relied on to defend Japan if doing so might provoke nuclear warfare. Other safeguards are needed. Accordingly, some in Japan advocate a rapid buildup of Japan's own self-defense forces, and a few have even suggested development of nuclear weapons. How Japan would deal with an ebbing of tension in East Asia would depend heavily on the state of Japan's own diplomatic relations with the Soviet Union and the People's Republic of China.

American Demands

Meantime, some American policy makers are raising new questions of their own.

End of the "Free Ride." Why, they are asking with growing insistence, should Japan continue to take a "free ride" on the coattails of U.S. military power? With an average per capita income the equal of that of the United States, with huge and growing current account surpluses and foreign exchange reserves, extraordinary industrial capacity, and a very low percentage of GNP devoted to defense (currently 0.9 percent compared with about 6 percent in the United States), why should the Japanese not accept a larger share of the burden for maintaining U.S. troops and bases in Japan?

Not all United States officials feel this way. The State Department is quick to point out that Japan actually is not taking a "free ride." U.S. bases in Japan cost Japanese taxpayers between $420 and $562 million during 1977, depending on how the costs are calculated, and perhaps as much as $600 million in 1978. Furthermore, Japan does maintain a respectable military force with primary responsibility for the immediate conventional defense of Japan, freeing the U.S. forces stationed in Japan for strategic or regional operations. And Japan will purchase in the near future about $6.5 billion worth of U.S. military equipment, including F-15 fighters and P-3C aircraft for antisubmarine warfare.

In view, however, of the economic problems facing the United States-Japanese alliance (discussed below)—the huge Japanese trade surpluses vis-à-vis the United States; rising demands in Congress for protection against Japanese exports; and the rapid appreciation of the yen, making even more costly the maintenance of American bases in Japan—it seems inevitable that the United States will apply heavy pressure on the government of Japan to take on a larger share of the cost of keeping American bases in Japan. The cost to American taxpayers of maintaining troops in Japan is somewhat more than $1 billion annually, and it rises rapidly each time the yen appreciates vis-à-vis the dollar. American pressure concerning base costs will, in turn, create difficulties for Japanese politicians, even those who strongly support the security treaty, since Diet members will have to explain to their constituents why they voted for more support for the unpopular American bases. No easy solution is in sight. The Japanese government hopes to deal quietly with the problem, and intense, behind-the-scenes negotiations have begun already. But it seems destined to become a major domestic political issue in time.

A Faster Military Buildup. Another problem will be the United States' insistence on a more rapid buildup of self-defense forces. For more than 20 years, American officials have been pushing their Japanese counterparts to speed up this process. The Japanese have retorted that they are going as fast as they can go, given the deeply rooted and widespread pacifism among the Japanese people. Japanese military forces are now deemed "respectable" by world standards. Japan's defense budget, about $10 billion in fiscal year 1978, exceeds the defense outlays of all United States' NATO allies except Britain, France, and Germany and is growing at about 12 percent each year. Nevertheless, United States military planners believe that Japan is not capable of defending itself against a large-scale conventional attack by the Soviet Union. Although the United States does not want to see Japan heavily armed or possessing nuclear weapons, it does intend to push Japan toward accepting responsibility for a somewhat wider defense perimeter, which will require more sophisticated and costly air and naval power. Conflict could thus arise over the pace of Japan's military buildup.

Arms Sales. Controversy on the domestic political scene over the extent to which Japan should produce its own weapons appears inevitable. Until now, because of popular mistrust of militarism, Japanese industry has refrained from producing arms up to its capacity, or exporting them, but the slow growth of the economy in recent years is creating pressures to produce arms on a larger scale. Should Japan decide to enter the arms sales business, it would be a formidable competitor.

The People's Republic of China could be a lucrative market for either Japanese or American arms. Some Japanese industries have already indicated an interest in developing that market, but both the Japanese government and public are still firmly opposed to such sales. The United States government has moved cautiously toward approval of sale to the Chinese of some equipment that has both military and civilian uses, such as infrared scanning devices, and may relax trade restrictions even further. There is thus the long-term potential of rivalry and friction between the United States and Japan over their respective policies in this field.

Plutonium

Japan's search for new sources of energy and American fears about nuclear proliferation have led the two countries into a serious impasse over development of fast-breeder plutonium reactors. Ever since the use of nuclear power for the generation of electricity became feasible, the United States has taken a benign, supportive view of Japan's development of peaceful nuclear technology. The United States demands controls and inspections and by treaty has asserted a claim to be the sole supplier of enriched uranium to Japan, but it welcomed, at least until 1977, any sign that the Japanese were overcoming their "nuclear allergy," born in the nightmare blasts at Hiroshima and Nagasaki.

With the oil crisis of 1973, Japan stepped up its efforts to develop alternative energy supplies. These efforts included the construction of a fast-breeder reactor which relies on plutonium for fuel and a reprocessing plant to create plutonium. Just as the Carter administration was coming into power in Washington, the Japanese were completing a facility at Tokaimura for reprocessing spent uranium fuel into plutonium.

Objecting to the introduction of plutonium into any country on the grounds that it could be converted into nuclear weapons, the Carter administration demanded in April 1977 that Japan cease work on the Tokaimura reactor and reprocessing plant. The Japanese were shocked and angered; the demand seemed an unwarranted intrusion into their domestic affairs, an ill-timed and ill-considered switch in American policy, and furthermore unnecessary in view of Japan's well-known aversion to nuclear weapons and stated policy of rejecting their manufacture or possession. Barring an unforeseen breakthrough in the development of new energy sources, the Japanese believe their economy will depend in some measure on plutonium power in the 1990s and beyond. In September 1977, after bitter wrangling, Prime Minister Fukuda and President Carter in effect postponed the dispute by agreeing to a two-year grace period during which Japan could operate Tokaimura to produce liquid plutonium nitrate, but not weapons-potential plutonium metal. Meanwhile, the two nations agreed that they would explore other forms of nuclear energy. But the question will arise again in 1979 and could cause a serious rift between the two nations if the United States clings to its position, and especially if it shuts off the supply of enriched uranium to Japan.

In rare defiance of American wishes, Japan signed long-term contracts with Britain and France in May 1978 under which spent nuclear fuel in Japan will be shipped to plants in Windscale, Britain, and LaHague, France, beginning in 1987, and brought back to Japan as plutonium for further use in fast-breeder reactors to provide electric power. Japanese power companies will invest more than $1 billion to finance the two reprocessing plants in France and Britain. Japan apparently will join efforts with several European nations to reject President Carter's appeal to forgo moving toward a "plutonium economy."

Legally, Japan owns whatever spent fuel is created when it burns enriched uranium imported from the United States. But under the agreement with Japan, the United States has the right to disapprove the extraction and transfer of plutonium from the spent fuel. In 1978, in withholding funds for the Clinch River fast-breeder reactor in Tennessee and for a reprocessing plant at Barnwell, South Carolina, that would extract plutonium from spent nuclear fuel, President Carter deferred indefinitely U.S. use of plutonium in hopes that the rest of the world would follow suit. The Japanese have informed the Carter administration that their economy depends on plutonium and, further, that they are running out of storage space for spent fuel, now kept in huge "swimming pools" of water near nuclear power plants, and thus have no choice but to reprocess it into plutonium. Japanese power companies had obtained Washington's permission in 1975 to ship spent fuel for reprocessing into plutonium to France and Britain, but they have not yet obtained the Carter administration's approval for the new contracts. They will need it by 1982 when construction is due to begin on the plants in Britain and France.

The Carter administration thus faces a major question in its dealings with Japan: Will it continue to reject plutonium for both the United States and other nations, and cut off Japan's supplies of enriched uranium, or will it drop its objections and approve Japan's plans to move to a plutonium economy?

Alaskan Oil

Another issue which Tokyo and Washington must settle involves Alaskan oil. So far the United States has refused to sell such oil to Japan. The

Japanese would like to buy the oil in order to avoid overdependence on Mideast oil supplies and to reduce their huge current account surplus with the United States. Under American law, the United States cannot sell Alaskan oil to any countries except Canada and Mexico. In 1977 the Carter administration considered trying to persuade the Congress to change the law in order to sell the oil to Japan, but dropped the idea "partly for political reasons," according to Energy Secretary James R. Schlesinger. The administration feared that the American people would not take the energy crisis seriously if the United States was exporting domestic oil to Japan.

Civil Aviation

Another irritant in relations is the current civil air agreement, signed in 1952, which the Japanese claim is an unequal hangover of the occupation mentality. Under the agreement, Japan Airlines (JAL) can land at Guam, Saipan, Anchorage, Honolulu, San Francisco, Los Angeles, and New York. American carriers can fly to Tokyo, Osaka, Okinawa, and beyond to Seoul, Hong Kong, and Taipei. JAL is seeking the right to pick up passengers at American airports such as Los Angeles or New York and fly them beyond, to South America, for example. JAL is also requesting the right to fly to other American cities such as Chicago and Seattle, and would like to serve passengers in Houston, Minneapolis, Kansas City, and Atlanta, who are flying on to Japan.

U.S. airlines object to opening up new portions of the domestic American market to the Japanese; they point out that Japan does not offer reciprocal rights to the Japanese market. Furthermore, the Japanese government is seeking to limit (1) the frequency of American flights which land in Tokyo and continue to third countries and (2) the number of passengers and amount of freight they can carry.

Negotiations on these matters, now in recess, are due to resume in late 1978 or early 1979.

The Trade Gap

The most serious problem presently facing the United States and Japan is their enormous and continuing current account imbalance, which has played havoc with attempts on both sides to encourage trade to grow in orderly stages for mutual advantage. The U.S. balance-of-payments deficit in 1977 vis-à-vis Japan was $8 billion, a record amount between the United States and any of its trading partners. (Overall, the American world balance-of-payments deficit was $15.2 billion, with imports of $44 billion of oil being the largest factor in the deficit.) The 1978 deficit vis-à-vis Japan may be even larger. Because of the continuing deficit, the value of the dollar against the yen fell to a new low and the yen rose to a new high in 1978. The dollar was falling well below 200 yen at mid-year compared with 360 when it was cut loose from a pegged rate in 1971, and 240 in late 1977. So rapid and dramatic a change in the value of the respective currencies raised disturbing new questions about future trade between the two countries, making it difficult in the short run for importers and exporters on both sides to make plans. In the long run, of course, such imbalances could not go on and would surely strengthen demands for a return to protectionism in the United States.

Causes. The problem has many causes, some deeply rooted in the economic systems of each nation. Japan, unlike the United States, traditionally has been an exporting state: the Japanese must sell manufactured goods abroad to pay for food, fuel, and materials (80 percent of its imports) in order to survive on the resource-poor home islands. Japanese corporations work closely with government ministries and the banks. They enjoy debt-equity ratios unheard of in the United States and have demonstrated perhaps more vigor and prowess than the world has ever seen in finding, studying, developing, and exploiting overseas markets. Japanese firms enjoy relatively strong support from labor unions, which accept changes in technology more readily than their American counterparts. Some small- and medium-sized Japanese firms pay slightly lower wage rates than comparable American firms, though wages in many large Japanese enterprises now equal or even surpass U.S. rates. In times of recession, such as from 1974 to 1975, Japanese firms beef up their export trade in order to maintain their system of lifetime employment of their workers; when sales slump on the domestic market, new export markets are sought overseas in order to meet the costs of this system, whereas in the United States workers would typically be laid off and receive unemployment compensation.

Japanese productivity, enhanced by the purchase of American and other foreign technology at relatively low prices since World War II and sustained by a highly educated, skilled, and motivated labor force, has risen to the point that other nations simply can no longer compete in certain product lines. With an unusually high rate of personal savings, capital has been abundant, and Japanese industry has invested it in the most modern, cost-saving equipment. One result has been that United States and other foreign steelmakers cannot easily compete with Japanese manufacturers. As part of their marketing strategy, Japanese firms sometimes sell products at lower prices abroad than at home; this has led to charges of "dumping" by U.S. firms whose sales have been hurt by the large volume of imported Japanese goods, such as television sets. Since the end of the occupation, Japanese governments have cooperated in the consolidation of firms in industries such as steel and shipbuilding in order to avoid excessive competition at home. This policy has prompted Americans to say that Japan is really "Japan Inc.," a giant corporation embracing the government, corporations, and unions. These charges are mostly unfair, a free-enterprise system with a relatively free market for most products operates in Japan at least as well as in the United States. But it must be added that Japanese business leaders, bureaucrats, and politicians tend to view problems from similar national perspectives and cooperate with each other more readily than do their American counterparts.

The enormous Japanese economic presence in the United States has many aspects, some positive, and some threatening. There can be no doubt that the high quality of Japanese television sets, watches, cars, cameras, and other consumer products has won the respect of millions of Americans. On the other hand, the Japanese have invested so heavily in land, timber, fisheries, agricultural enterprises, and other industrial facilities, particularly in the five Pacific states of Hawaii, Alaska, Oregon, Washington, and California, that there is a feeling among some Americans that they are parts of "resource colony" for an expanding Japanese economic empire.

Despite this investment in the United States, the balance-of-payments surplus for Japan continued to grow dramatically in 1977-1978. One of the reasons is that American exports in the past five years have been losing their share of the Japanese market.

In 1977 Japan exported more than $19 billion worth of goods to the United States but imported just under $12 billion worth of American products. There are many reasons for this. American firms, with some notable exceptions, have not traditionally been "export-oriented" and by and large do not perform as well overseas as their Japanese counterparts. Japan, moreover, has traditionally protected its domestic market from imports which could hurt certain important political constituencies, such as farmers.

Japan also has strict laws on foreign investment, which tend to curb the flow of American capital into the country. For a time after World War II the United States accepted a high degree of Japanese protectionism as the only means of restoring infant or recovering industries to economic health. But the restrictions—tariffs, quotas, and red tape—have persisted long after their purpose was served, and they prevented American exports of beef and agricultural goods such as citrus fruits from flowing onto the Japanese market, where there is a ready demand. The restrictions have been eased considerably in recent years, but even the remaining ones cause considerable irritation because of the growing trade gap.

A Negotiated Agreement. When the startling extent of the 1977 trade imbalance became clear late in the year, emergency negotiations were launched between teams headed by President Carter's special trade representative,

Robert S. Strauss, and special envoy Nobuhiko Ushiba, a highly respected former Japanese ambassador to Washington. The talks were long and heated. The Americans complained that the Japanese economy had failed in recent years to grow at the hoped-for and promised rate of 7 percent and urged Japan to stimulate higher growth through deficit financing and more public works projects. Higher growth, it was argued, would lead to increased demand for American products. The Americans also urged further liberalization of Japan's remaining trade restrictions, including hidden restraints, and closer scrutiny of Japan's export practices. They talked of Japan's "free ride" on defense and consequent obligation to cooperate more in the economic sphere.

The Japanese contended that the U.S. current account deficit in international trade was caused mainly by its inability or unwillingness to curb imports of foreign oil, rather than its deficit toward Japan. As for national defense, the Japanese argued that it was an American decision to shoulder the major burden. The Japanese pointed out that they could enter the arms sales race and compete very effectively against American products, but had deliberately refrained from doing so. The Japanese noted that many American products were not attractive to Japanese consumers and urged that American exporters study Japanese markets with more care. They noted that the rate of inflation in Japan had been brought down to 2 percent as compared with 6 percent or more in the United States. The United States, they said, must learn to control inflation at home if it is to remain competitive abroad. As adherents of a free-enterprise economy, they added, the Japanese government simply could not order Japanese exporters to curb their activities and importers to increase their purchases.

The talks resulted in the Strauss-Ushiba Agreement of January 13, 1978. The agreement, completed in Tokyo after frantic, all-night negotiations which constantly threatened to come apart at the seams, provided that Japan would take steps to achieve a "marked diminution" in 1978 of its present current account surplus and thereafter would make "all reasonable efforts" to achieve further reductions "aiming at equilibrium, with deficit accepted if it should occur." For its part, the United States promised to attempt to curb inflation, increase exports, and to reduce its dependence on oil imports; Strauss gave his personal expression of confidence that Congress would pass an effective energy program.

The Strauss-Ushiba communiqué also added language designed to achieve parity in United States-Japan trading relationships. Japan and the United States agreed to try to set "comparable levels of bound tariffs." This meant that Japan would negotiate future tariff cuts in terms of the actual tariff structure, and not, as in the past, in terms of some theoretical level above the actual level.

Japan also undertook to increase import quotas on beef, citrus fruits, and other products; to review and liberalize foreign exchange controls; to send Japanese buying missions to the United States; and to end bureaucratic nontariff barriers, promising that any remaining barriers could be monitored through a Joint Trade Facilitation Committee.

In connection with the negotiations, the Japanese government publicly announced a target of 7 percent growth rate for 1978, well above the actual 5.3 percent in 1977, and abandonment of the custom that no more than 30 percent of the budget could be financed by borrowing (postwar Japanese governments customarily have not resorted to deficit financing). The goal of 7 percent growth fits in well with the Carter administration's hope that Japan and West Germany, together with the United States, would serve as "locomotive" economies in pulling the West from the economic doldrums which began with the recession of 1974-1975.

But the results of all this in 1978 have not been promising, and the trade gap seems likely to worsen. Japanese exports were declining slightly in volume, but because of the shift in the yen-dollar rate were listed at a much higher dollar value. As the dollar fell in relation to the yen, the price of Japanese imports into the United States rose accordingly. But this seemed to have little effect on American consumers; they continued to buy Japanese automobiles and other products in record amounts, with only a few exceptions. At some point, the higher prices of Japanese imports were certain to turn away some American customers and thus ease the trade gap. But demand for Japanese products showed surprising strength despite their higher cost to Americans. American automakers failed to take advantage of the opportunity to undersell the small Japanese cars; they simply raised their prices to the new level of imports.

Japanese leaders began to give voice to criticisms which have been felt for several years—that American industry is growing weak and non-competitive, that American workers are habitually lazy, and that the American government has lost its ability to control inflation and stimulate productivity. In short, the Japanese raised new questions about the reliability and wisdom of their economic dependence on the United States and stepped up their search for alternatives.

Japan's only other alliance with a Western power—the Anglo-Japanese alliance of 1902—lasted just 19 years. The United States-Japanese alliance is still strong after more than a quarter of a century, and both nations see their own national interests, military, political, and economic, served well by it. In light of this, perhaps not too much should be made of these problems. But it is also worth remembering that the alliance has been managed by an extraordinarily knowledgeable and sensitive corps of diplomats, bureaucrats, and military men on both sides who are solid believers in its values, who share experiences dating back to the occupation, and who are skilled in mediating its tensions. As new generations of leaders move into power in each country—leaders who have not shared the occupation experience—will they be able to deal as well with the new tensions and problems that lie in the uncharted waters of the 1980s and beyond?

Notes

1. White Paper on Defense (Summary), *Defense Bulletin*, Public Information Division, Defense Agency, vol. 1, no. 3, September 1977. Cited by Bernard K. Gordon in "Japan, the United States and Southeast Asia," *Foreign Affairs*, April 1978, pp. 579-80.

2 American Perceptions

Relations between the United States and Japan depend not only on the underlying realities but also on the view of the American people. How do Americans perceive the current state of ties between the countries? What do Americans think of the Japanese and of certain policies of the Japanese government? How supportive are Americans of our military commitments to Japan? Compared with other countries, where does Japan rank in importance to Americans?

To get at some of these matters, a special survey of attitudes of Americans toward Japan was commissioned in mid-April 1978 by Potomac Associates. The survey also included some comparative questions designed to determine public priorities among Japan and other nations on a global scale.

Summary of Views on Japan

As regards Japan, the results can be summarized as follows: The citizens of the United States appear quite knowledgeable about Japan and generally hold Japan and the Japanese people in high regard. Many of the negative stereotypes prevalent in the era of World War II have given way to a markedly positive image of Japan.

Most Americans support maintaining the U.S. troop level in Japan at current levels or higher. Further, at least one American in two favors coming to the defense of Japan with U.S. military might, should Japan be attacked by either the Soviet Union or the People's Republic of China.

Americans look on Japan as a reliable friend, and rank it near the top of the list as a nation important to U.S. global interests.

Only concern in the minds of many Americans about the trade imbalance and its perceived effects on unemployment in the United States clouds the picture.

This largely supportive public mood provides considerable leverage for President Carter and his foreign policy advisers in addressing some of the outstanding problems between the United States and Japan. The administration, in negotiating with Japan over the formulation of mutually supportive policies, need not fear a public backlash against some degree of U.S. pressure on Japan to alleviate the serious trade balance problem. Indeed, failure to deal successfully with that problem could heighten protectionist sentiment among the public at large and exaggerate protectionist pressures that already exist in Congress and among various special interest groups in this country.

It is important, we believe, that Japanese policy makers pay as much attention to this last point as their American counterparts. The generally warm view of Americans toward Japan and the Japanese holds much promise for the future. But this condition could be dissipated by an uncritical acceptance of the positive, and a failure to deal with those negatives that could sour the public outlook, and generate a strong anti-Japanese trend both in the public at large and among their representatives on Capitol Hill.

We do not suggest that policy should be made solely on the basis of popular moods. Frequently the challenge to leadership is to have the wisdom and courage to take actions that run counter to prevailing public sentiment. But it is also true that citizens can, in their collective outlook, provide some useful and even compelling reactions that political leadership would be well advised to take into account. The shape of public opinion can have both a limiting and a directing effect on how our national leaders act. It can indicate as well to those leaders the degree of public education needed before a workable consensus can be built around new policy approaches. This is particularly true in the current post-Vietnam and post-Watergate atmosphere, when the elected representatives in Congress are playing a larger role in the conduct of foreign policy than they have for many years, and when the public is more skeptical of many national institutions—including the presidency and Congress—than it once was.

Importance of Europe versus Asia

Before we turn to some specific issues involving the United States and Japan, let us look at how Americans respond to some questions that are global in scope. We first asked our sample to weigh the relative importance of Europe and Asia:

> The United States has strong political, economic, and national defense ties with friendly nations in Western Europe on one hand, and with friendly nations in and near Asia, on the other hand. Thinking about each of these two areas from the standpoint of promoting our own political, economic, and national defense interests, which one do you think is more important to the United States, friendly nations in Western Europe or friendly nations in Asia?

Friendly nations in Western Europe	39%
Friendly nations in Asia	18
Both equally important	29
Don't know	14

Clearly, those Americans who choose one geographic area over another look to Europe as the locus of principal American interests, by a margin of more than 2 to 1. Yet almost three Americans in ten see both as equally important. That Europe should rank ahead of Asia is not particularly surprising, given the strong cultural and historical ties that cross the Atlantic and the fact that the vast majority of Americans trace their ancestry to the European continent. What may, in fact, be most significant in these figures is that the imbalance between Europe and Asia is not greater and that so many Americans see both areas of roughly equal importance. The American people do not see our national interests tied exclusively, or even predominantly, to a single portion of the world.

The national data have been broken down by sex, age, education, politics, and region. Groups in the population do not differ much in their views on this question. People 18 to 29 years of age see nations in Asia as more important than does any other group. While 37 percent of the young regard Western European countries as primary, 27 percent rate Asia first. Another 26 percent see both as equal. Perhaps this sense of Asia's relative importance among the younger generation stems from a more direct feeling of involvement in the war in Vietnam, as well as the attraction that Asian philosophy and the emergence on the international scene of the People's Republic of China have for many younger Americans. Except for this minor variation, the overall distribution of opinion is the same in all groups: Europe first in importance, followed by Europe and Asia as equally important areas, and Asia third.

Importance of Individual Countries

What about individual countries? How do Americans sort out their priorities when they are asked to rate the relative importance of relations with an array of nations around the globe? We asked our cross section of the American people to give their views on 14 countries:

When it comes to pursuing our interests all around the world, how important do you think it is for the U.S. to try to get along well with each of the following countries—very important, fairly important, not so important, or not important at all?

Adding those who answer "very important" and "fairly important" for each country produces the following ranking:

	Very Important or Fairly Important
Canada	88 percent
Soviet Union	86
Japan	86
West Germany	85
Saudi Arabia	82
Israel	81
Egypt	78
People's Republic of China on the mainland	77
Republic of China on Taiwan	72
Brazil	66
India	65
Cuba	64
South Korea	62
North Korea	51

This question was not designed to get a sense of relative warmth or friendliness toward these countries. Prior studies have made clear that this would have resulted in a substantially different ranking; the Soviet Union would have placed much lower in the esteem of Americans, for example, and the Republic of China on Taiwan would have stood ahead of the People's Republic on the mainland.[1] Such popularity contests have an interest of their own, but they do not tell much to the policy maker or policy analyst. What does a general sense of goodwill toward a given country mean, for example, in a period when national interests may diverge?

Even though attitudes toward the Soviet Union have hardened in the wake of complications over completion of a SALT II agreement and the trial and conviction of a number of Soviet dissidents, Americans have remained firm in their view that the United States should continue to negotiate with the Soviet Union and that efforts should be made to conclude a mutually beneficial arms agreement. It was precisely such *apparent* conflicts in outlook that we wished to discover, by asking Americans to assess the importance of relations with countries not on the basis of friendship and good will but according to how vital they see these nations to U.S. interests. The very fact that the public rates the Soviet Union, our principal adversary in today's world, second only to Canada—a nation sometimes pictured as taken for granted by Americans but with which we share an open border and many basic goals to a degree perhaps unsurpassed anywhere else on the globe—suggests Americans observe the world around them with a fair measure of sophistication and good sense. A good friend and a dedicated opponent can be seen as near equals in terms of their relative importance to our national interests.

Overall Ratings

Let us discuss the countries on the list in descending order of ranking. The high ratings given to both Japan and West Germany, former bitter American enemies but now close allies, no doubt reflect their enormous economic and strategic importance to the United States. Each, presumably, is seen as a bulwark in their part of the world, linked to U.S. political, security, and economic objectives in many ways.

That Saudi Arabia is the next country on our list—it actually ranks marginally ahead of Japan among those who say it is very important—shows how quickly public opinion can shift in a rapidly changing international environment. Although there are no earlier data with which to contrast these findings, surely it is safe to say that the importance of Saudi Arabia has climbed dramatically in the public eye as the realities of our energy needs and our dependence on the Saudis have impinged on American consciousness. It is also worth noting that Saudi Arabia, Israel, and Egypt are clustered together in terms of their perceived importance to U.S. interests—just as they were linked in the recent Carter administration arms sale package.

It was noted earlier that the Republic of China on Taiwan invariably stands well ahead of the People's Republic on the mainland when Americans rate them in terms of favorable or unfavorable attitudes. But when the notion of pursuing U.S. policy objectives is introduced, the picture is reversed. Instead, it is the People's Republic that comes first, almost certainly a recognition on the part of Americans of the disparity in size, power, and potential influence between the two claimants to Chinese leadership. Perhaps the American people have come to understand both the possibility and even the logic of a changed set of ties between Washington, Peking, and Taipei, and have given an implicit indication of approval to a new international reality.

That Brazil, India, and Cuba, the next three countries on the list, rank relatively low does not come as a major surprise. Brazil, the largest and one of the most important nations in Latin America, almost surely is taken for granted simply because it is in Latin America. India is probably seen as a nation beset by so many internal problems and so unpredictable in its international orientation that it, too, is not held central to U.S. interests. Cuba, in spite of its highly publicized activities in Africa and the tentative steps in 1977 between Washington and Havana toward improved bilateral ties, does not command primary attention from Americans. Many observers would argue that this assessment is roughly appropriate to the true level of U.S. interests vis-à-vis Cuba, particularly as long as the issues that separate the two countries show little prospect of resolution and larger problems elsewhere demand more urgent attention.

   With the possible exception of the high ranking given to Saudi Arabia, the most intriguing and, we believe, disturbing result of this part of our survey is the low level of importance given to South Korea relative to U.S. objectives around the globe. That North Korea should come last is logical, since it is rarely in the news and probably is seen as playing a minor role in world affairs. But South Korea is another matter. After all, other data derived from our survey indicate that a majority of Americans have serious doubts about President Carter's plan for withdrawal of troops from South Korea. The perceived importance of South Korea to U.S. interests undoubtedly has been hard hit by the "Koreagate" scandal, and perhaps by concern that South Korea's exposed position, and our commitment to its security, could involve the United States in another land war in Asia—a prospect uncongenial to the American people in the aftermath of the Vietnam war.

Variations among Groups

It is striking how small the variations were on this question among different demographic subgroups. In the case of Japan, Americans with a college education are most supportive of efforts to develop good relations: 94 percent feel this way, and 61 percent say it is very important, the largest percentage of any single group holding that view. This strong backing from the college-educated, who tend to be better informed on foreign policy issues than others and who also are one of the most influential groups in our society because of their greater professional access to positions of power and decision making, should be encouraging to those who wish to see close relations between Tokyo and Washington.
   In the case of South and North Korea, Americans 65 years and above are less convinced than the nation as a whole of the importance of good ties; in both instances, however, this is accounted for by the larger numbers in this age group who have no opinion. Otherwise, outlooks among demographic subgroups conform quite closely to overall totals.
   The same condition applies to the Republic of China on Taiwan. Even political affiliation does not seem to affect views on the relative importance of good relations with Taiwan. Given the occasionally heated nature of political debate on the China issue, debate in which Republicans more often than not have been the staunchest supporters of Taiwan, one might have thought that political persuasion would play a more determining role here.
   Age affects attitudes concerning the People's Republic of China. The elderly see less at stake: 67 percent say that good relations are either very important or fairly important, compared with the overall total of 77 percent. Again, this is largely accounted for by a high percentage of "don't knows."

More than any other group, Americans 18 to 29 years of age believe relations with the People's Republic are very important—50 percent, as compared to the national average of 43 percent. It will be recalled that young Americans are more inclined than any other group to see friendly countries in Asia as more important to U.S. interests than friendly countries in Western Europe. While these views are not exactly parallel, they suggest a particular affinity for Asia in the minds of this generation.

As with Japan, the college-educated are most interested in seeing the United States get along well with the People's Republic: 83 percent rank this very important or fairly important. This provides a backdrop of understanding from a key segment of the American population for continuing, albeit at times sporadic, efforts since the Nixon breakthrough to improve relations with the world's most populous country.

Some Conclusions

A review of this particular set of findings leads to at least three general conclusions. The first is the relative homogeneity of American outlooks on the relative importance of various countries to perceived U.S. interests, whether these countries are friendly, unfriendly, or somewhere in between. It can be argued that this is partially a result of the degree to which most Americans get their news—especially on international affairs—from a limited number of sources, most of which tend to select what is news and to present events in reasonably similar fashion. International reporting by the major television networks, principal news weeklies, those daily newspapers that devote much space to foreign affairs, and the wire services is not all that different in tone. And so it is understandable that Americans have a great deal in common when making the kind of broad judgments that this part of our survey elicited. Whatever the cause, this relative homogeneity means that policy makers and those who try to influence policy are dealing with a public that is reasonably predictable.

The second conclusion runs somewhat counter to the first. Substantial numbers of Americans answer "don't know" when asked questions about events on the international scene. From the standpoint of the policy maker, this portion of the populace—which is markedly larger than on surveys about domestic affairs—represents a target for public education, a reservoir of opinion that can be channeled in one direction or another through sensible argument, emotional appeal, or the force of unfolding events.

Third, we conclude that the order in which Americans rank the relative importance to the United States of the fourteen nations on the list shows generally solid judgment. Experts in one field or another or supporters of certain countries or interests might prefer a different ranking. But, overall, the outcome reflects a level of realism, sophistication, and pragmatic good sense that tends to belie the notion that Americans are woefully ignorant about the world beyond their borders and naive in assessing national interests. That blind spots exist, some serious, is indisputable. Other parts of our survey will reveal some of these. But our overall conclusion, we believe, is sustainable and reassuring.

Defense of U.S. Allies

As a world leader, the United States bears a particular responsibility for the maintenance of international peace and stability. In the aftermath of the Vietnam war, the emergence of other major power centers, and the growing complexity of the international arena, this role appears to be one the American people are now generally perceived as unwilling—or at least less willing—to assume. This is almost certainly the case if it means involvement in ventures abroad that could lead to armed conflict and the commitment of U.S. forces where the rationale is neither clear nor persuasive.

But does this mean that Americans are not prepared to come to the defense of friends and allies under any circumstances? To find out, we repeated in our April 1978 survey a line of inquiry that we had used in part before. This permits us to see not only where Americans stand now but also whether their views have shifted.

Please tell me whether you agree or disagree with the following statements.

The United States should come to the defense of its major European allies with military force if any of them are attacked by Soviet Russia.

	1972	1974	1975	1976	1978
Agree	52%	48%	48%	56%	62%
Disagree	32	34	34	27	26
Don't know	16	18	18	17	12

The United States should come to the defense of Japan with military force if it is attacked by Soviet Russia or Communist China.

	1972	1974	1975	1976	1978
Agree	43%	37%	42%	45%	50%
Disagree	40	42	39	37	35
Don't know	17	21	19	18	15

The United States should come to the defense of South Korea with military force if it is attacked by North Korea.

	1978 (Not asked in previous years)
Agree	32%
Disagree	52
Don't know	16

The United States should come to the defense of the Republic of China on Taiwan with military force if it is attacked by Communist China from the mainland.

	1977a	1978
Agree	36%	32%
Disagree	40	48
Don't know	24	20

aThe wording of the 1977 question was substantially different and may have elicited a slightly more positive response: "Suppose the United States broke off diplomatic and defense treaty relations with the Republic of China on Taiwan, and established full diplomatic relations with Mainland China, on the assumption that Mainland China would not use force against Taiwan. And suppose further that sometime later Mainland China attacked Taiwan in order to take it over. Would you favor or oppose the U.S. coming directly to the defense of Taiwan with our naval and air forces?"

The particular importance the public attaches to U.S. interests vis-à-vis Japan and West Germany, as noted in the preceding section, is clearly reflected in these expressions of Americans' willingness to defend certain of our allies. Indeed, in the case of both Japan and "major European allies," the percentage of Americans who agree that we should support them with military force in the event of attack by communist powers has moved steadily upward over the past four years and is now at its highest level since we initiated this particular series of questions. This is probably explained by growing concern about a perceived Soviet threat, greater worry about the menace of communism, and enhanced fear of war among Americans, all of which have been documented in other Potomac Associates studies.[2] This trend of support for Japan and our European allies continues unabated, with Europe coming first, in keeping with the primacy accorded Europe over Asia that was discussed earlier.

Among demographic groups, men, Republicans, the college-educated, and those aged 30 to 49 are the most supportive of military action in the case of attack on either Japan or our major European allies. In the case of Europe, 70 percent of the male population would back such action versus only 55 percent of women. So would 67 percent of those 30 to 49 years of age, 71 percent of the Republicans, and 70 percent of those with a college education.

When the question was posed about defending Japan, the comparable figures are 61 percent of the men, 56 percent of those 30 to 49 years of age, 57 percent of the Republicans, and 60 percent of the college-educated. Variations in opinion based on region of the country are insignificant in regard to defending either Japan or Europe.

Support for South Korea and the Republic of China on Taiwan is markedly lower. In fact, a majority *opposes* coming to the defense of South Korea in the event of another attack from the north, and a plurality is against defense of Taiwan should it come under attack from the mainland. Once again, men, Republicans, the college-educated, and those aged 30 to 49 rank highest in their support for both South Korea and Taiwan, but in no group is even a plurality in favor of military intervention.

This is obviously bad news for friends and supporters of South Korea and Taiwan. In the case of Korea, however, such opposition to future engagement in hostilities is not translated into a desire to have U.S. troops removed at present, as we shall discuss shortly. But it does appear that "Koreagate" and questions about limitations on human rights may have taken a toll in public support for military engagement.

It also appears that the gradual improvement of relations between the United States and the People's Republic of China has moved a substantial proportion of the American people to oppose combat involvement in the event of a future clash between the mainland and Taiwan. It may be that after Vietnam, the specter of another land war in Asia (the public may assume that U.S. defense of Taiwan might include actions against the mainland) makes more Americans unwilling to assume such a burden than to support it.

Under such circumstances, the fact that half of the American people, and majorities among some groups, favor military defense of Japan in case of attack is all the more significant. Japan's perceived role as a world power and its economic and other major links to the United States give it a special place in the minds of Americans. Do we see here the drawing of an implicit defense perimeter in the minds of Americans—a security-based "trilateralism" writ large?

Reliability of Asian Nations

The great discrepancy in American willingness to defend various countries if attacked, in particular the contrast between support for Japan and for South Korea, may well be related to how reliable Americans feel these countries are. To test this hypothesis, we asked:

When you think about Asia, which of the countries listed on this card is in your own view, our most *reliable friend in that part of the world?*

Japan	48%
Republic of China	12
India	11
South Korea	9
Don't know	20

And which of these countries is the least *reliable?*

Japan	7%
Republic of China	21
South Korea	21
India	26
Don't know	25

On both counts, Japan fares far better than any other country. This is especially true among the college-educated, 60 percent of whom regard it as our most reliable friend. Americans 65 or older are among the most restrained toward Japan: only 40 percent think it the most reliable. Perhaps their memories of World War II are particularly strong. Even in their minds, however, Japan is seen as considerably more reliable than the other countries mentioned.

The poor rating of the reliability of both the Republic of Korea and the Republic of China almost certainly helps explain the reluctance of our respondents to defend them if these countries are attacked. They also suffer by being compared to Japan, which ranks so high in the eyes of Americans on all measurements assessed thus far. When most Americans look to Asia, their most positive thoughts are reserved for Japan.

U.S. Troop Levels Abroad

Future contingencies notwithstanding, how do Americans feel about the mission of U.S. forces stationed abroad? Should these troops be brought home, should they be left as is, or should their numbers be increased? Here are the results to queries posed in our April 1978 survey, with some limited comparative data.

As you probably know, the United States now has substantial military forces stationed in Western Europe for defense purposes. Under present circumstances, do you think the commitment of American forces in Europe should be increased, kept at the present level, reduced, or ended altogether?

	1972[b]	1974	1978
Increased	6%	3%	9%
Kept at present level	44	52	59
Reduced	30	25	14
Ended altogether	15	12	9
Don't know	5	8	9

The United States also has substantial forces stationed in Asia for defense purposes, including Japan and South Korea. Under present circumstances do you think the commitment of American forces in Japan should be increased, kept at the present level, reduced, or ended altogether?

	(Not asked in 1972)	1974 (Asia as a whole)[c]	1978
Increased		5%	6%
Kept at present level		54	58
Reduced		23	15
Ended altogether		12	11
Don't know		6	10

And what about South Korea? Should the commitment of American forces there be increased, kept at the present level, reduced, or ended altogether?

	(Not asked in 1972)	1974 (Asia as a whole)[c]	1978
Increased		5%	6%
Kept at present level		54	49
Reduced		23	17
Ended altogether		12	17
Don't know		6	11

[b]The wording of the question in 1972 was slightly different: "As you may know, the United States now has substantial military forces stationed in Western Europe as part of NATO's defense against the danger of Soviet aggression. Do you think America's contribution of ground troops now serving in Europe should be increased, kept at the present level, reduced, or ended altogether?"

[c]The wording of the question in 1974 was also different: "The United States also has substantial military forces stationed in Asia for defense purposes, including in Japan, South Korea, and Thailand. Under present circumstances, do you think the commitment of American forces in Asia should be increased, kept at the present level, reduced, or ended altogether?"

In looking first at the 1978 responses, the most important fact to note is that in all three instances a clear majority of Americans wants U.S. force commitments either kept at the present level or increased. Almost seven Americans in ten (68 percent) feel this way in the case of Europe; 64 percent concerning Japan; and 55 percent in regard to South Korea. While the figures concerning Japan and Europe are fully understandable in light of

American willingness to come to their defense in case of attack, the Korean data are somewhat surprising: they conflict with the expressed reluctance of Americans to defend South Korea against attack from the north. Perhaps the answer is to be found in the belief that since the peace-keeping role of U.S. forces in South Korea has proved effective thus far, why risk the consequences of troop withdrawal? Thus, a majority of Americans can oppose involvement in new hostilities, should they break out, and at the same time favor keeping our troops there to prevent hostilities from occurring.

Because some of the questions in earlier years that touch on this subject contained slightly different wording, exact comparisons are not always possible. But it is certainly fair to say that support for current or increased U.S. troop levels in Europe has risen in recent years, has apparently done the same in the case of Japan, and seems to have undergone only a marginal decline in regard to South Korea. While Americans may be more selective in choosing those countries they would wish to defend in the event of attack, they do not show any signs of wanting to remove the protective American troop shield around the world and to retreat to a fortress America.

Against this backdrop of favorable attitudes toward Japan, compared with other countries on certain broad political and security related matters, let us now analyze responses to questions dealing with Japan directly.

Knowledge of Japan

To begin, we wanted to find out something about the American level of awareness about Japan and the Japanese and how Americans get their information about Japan.

Geographic Location

Do Americans, for example, have an accurate picture of Japan's geographic location?

Which one of these statements about Japan is correct?

Japan has a common land boundary with the Soviet Union.	8%
Japan has a common land boundary with India	2
Japan is a nation of islands.	58
Japan has a common land boundary with Communist China.	20
Don't know.	12

Almost six Americans in ten (58 percent) realize that Japan is a nation of islands. The college-educated and those who live in the West are the best informed (78 and 75 percent, respectively). The fact that another 20 percent believe that Japan has a common land boundary with the People's Republic of China may well be of more than passing significance. To the extent that these people see Japan as a friend and China as an adversary, their feelings of support for Japan could be enhanced by their belief it lies next to a communist giant.

Japanese Products

In another test of knowledge, we asked whether a number of products sold widely in the United States are Japanese- or American-produced.

Here on this card is a list of American and Japanese brand names of products sold to the American consumer. Please tell me which ones you recognize as American and which as Japanese?

	American	Japanese	Don't know
Sony	10%	78%	12%
Zenith	81	9	10
Panasonic	29	53	18
Motorola	77	11	12
Datsun	9	76	15
Honda	12	75	13
Nikon	3	75	22
Polaroid	78	10	12

Approximately eight Americans in ten correctly identify every product but one as either American or Japanese. The one exception—Panasonic, about which slightly more than half are correct (almost three in ten think it is American)—may be due to the fact that the name itself has an American ring to it. Furthermore, advertising for Japanese products in this country does not stress that such products are Japanese, unlike, for example, the prominence given to the German manufacture of many German products. Perhaps Japanese producers have an innate modesty or concern about Americans' memories of World War II. They also may fear that an earlier stereotype about shoddy Japanese products will harm sales. If so, their assumption is mistaken, as we shall see when we examine current American stereotypes about the Japanese.

It is worth noting that throughout the Japan portion of the survey, men and the college-educated proved among the most knowledgeable, particularly in the identification of Japanese products. Americans 65 years old and over and those with only a grade school education are the least informed. In addition, a large number of these two groups express no opinion on questions about Japan.

Trade Imbalance

We also tested awareness of the current trade imbalance between the two countries, one of the most acute issues facing negotiators.

Is it your impression that the United States now sells more goods to Japan than it buys, does the United States buy more goods from Japan than it sells, or are sales between the United States and Japan about equal?

U.S. sells more than it buys.	5%
U.S. buys more than it sells.	70
U.S. buys and sells equally.	13
Don't know	12

A scant 5 percent of the respondents are under the illusion that the United States is the net beneficiary in the trade balance. Once again, men and the college-educated are well informed, with 75 percent and 78 percent, respectively, realizing that the United States buys more from Japan than it sells. Westerners turn out to be the most knowledgeable of all; 81 percent respond correctly. Presumably, their Pacific orientation and the entry of Japanese products through their part of the country have added to their awareness.

Sources of Information

Finally, we asked people to identify their main sources of information about Japan.

Of the following, which are your main sources of awareness about Japan? Please pick the one or two most important to you.

Television and radio	65%
Newspapers, magazines, and books	53
Movies	4
Purchase and use of Japanese goods	18
Personal contacts with Japanese	9
Don't know	6

Clearly, the media, other than movies, are the most influential. Television and radio are particularly important to people with either a high school or a grade school education: 68 and 73 percent of these groups, respectively, mention broadcasting, whereas 52 and 34 percent, respectively, mention newspapers, magazines, and books. On the other hand, reading materials are more influential for the college-educated: 68 percent mention them while 53 percent mention television and radio. Also of interest is the substantial number of Americans who point to purchase and use of Japanese goods; close to one in five (18 percent) mentions this as a principal source of awareness. And while only one American in eleven (9 percent) says that personal contacts with Japanese provide a major source of information, almost double that proportion of Westerners (17 percent) cite such contacts.

General Impressions of Japan and the Japanese

These responses suggest Americans are fairly well informed about at least a few basic matters relating to Japan. What, then, are their overall attitudes toward the country and its people? We saw earlier that Japan rates well in comparison with a number of other countries. But what about the more specific views of Americans on U.S.-Japanese relations and visceral feelings about the Japanese character? A number of questions in our survey dealt with these issues.

Popularity

One question probed general attitudes toward Japan; comparable figures are included for South and North Korea, obtained during our April 1978 survey, and for the Republic of China on Taiwan and the People's Republic of China on the mainland, obtained in an earlier Potomac Associates survey conducted in April 1977.

	Japan	South Korea	North Korea	Republic of China	People's Republic of China
Very favorable	22%	7%	1%	15%	4%
Somewhat favorable	50	45	12	41	22
Somewhat unfavorable	13	20	35	13	29
Very unfavorable	4	7	30	5	23
Don't know	11	21	22	26	22

As expected, given other findings discussed earlier, Japan clearly stands at the head of the line; Taiwan, South Korea, China, and North Korea follow in that order. The college-educated and Westerners are particularly positive in their attitudes toward Japan, 81 percent and 84 percent, respectively, viewing Japan either very or somewhat favorably.

What underlies this strikingly favorable outlook toward Japan? We have seen already that Americans view Japan as crucial to U.S. global interests, but that cannot be the only reason; the Soviet Union is also seen in that light, but the Soviet Union is far less popular among Americans.[3]

Character Traits

One approach is to look for a sense of how Americans see the Japanese as people. What character traits do Americans ascribe to individual Japanese? With this in mind, we asked our respondents to choose between paired words or phrases that might be used to describe the Japanese. In order to minimize bias in the interview, sometimes the more positive term in a pair was mentioned first and sometimes the more negative one. The word or phrase in each pair which was chosen most frequently is listed in the first column.

Loyal	55%	Treacherous	35%	Don't know	10%
Sly	54	Open	37		9
Competitive	80	Acquiescent	9		11
Hard-working	87	Lazy	4		9
Kind	56	Cruel	30		14
Light-skinned	57	Dark-skinned	32		11
Disciplined	82	Undisciplined	8		10
Intelligent	85	Dull	6		9
Up-to-date	76	Behind-the-times	14		10
Conservative	64	Radical	24		12
Humble	50	Arrogant	37		13
Group-oriented	73	Individualistic	17		10
Straightforward	50	Deceitful	37		13
Polite	79	Rude	10		11
Peaceful	58	Warlike	30		12
Democratic	49	Totalitarian	35		16
Short	88	Tall	2		10
Religious	65	Atheistic	22		13
Producers of good products	68	Producers of shoddy products	21		11
Creative	64	Imitative	26		10
Clean	77	Dirty	11		12
Brave	80	Cowardly	9		11

With few exceptions, a dramatically positive image of the Japanese emerges. Of all the pairings where one term could be construed as definitely negative, only the majority choice of "sly" over "open" stands out, and this is partially offset by the preference for "straightforward" as opposed to "deceitful." Worth special mention is the view of Japanese as "up-to-date," "creative," and "producers of good products," all of which stand in sharp contrast to the caricature of Japanese common before World War II as an imitative and somewhat backward people who produced toys that always broke. Now they are seen as hard-working and intelligent, disciplined and peaceful, loyal and kind. Taken as a whole, this is a picture of a people that would understandably lead Americans to regard their nation in favorable terms.

Among demographic subgroups, a few patterns emerge. Men are more positive in their views of Japanese than women. The college-educated are consistently the most positive of any group. Westerners, because of their greater orientation to Asia, are more complimentary than people living elsewhere in the country, while Southerners tend to be the most negative among regional groups. Younger Americans, 18 to 29, are more positive than their elders; those 65 years of age and older, whose memories of World War II may be especially strong, are among the most negative.

U.S.-Japanese Relations

Not only do most Americans hold the Japanese in high regard, but also they believe that relations between the two countries are good and prospects for the future are not bad.

Do you feel that at the present time relations between the United States and Japan are excellent, good, only fair, or poor?

Excellent	8%
Good	52
Only fair	28
Poor	3
Don't know	9

Over the next few years, do you expect relations between the United States and Japan to get better, get worse, or stay about the same as they are now?

Get better	21%
Stay about the same	54
Get worse	14
Don't know	11

The pattern of viewing Japan in a favorable light continues to hold true. Only 3 percent of the public see current relations as poor, and 60 percent view them as good or excellent. Once again, the college-educated and Westerners are the most positive, 73 percent of both groups viewing present relations as either good or excellent. Republicans are almost as positive (70 percent); Democrats and Independents are less so (58 and 59 percent, respectively).

Looking to the future, the preponderance of opinion is that relations between the United States and Japan will remain about the same as they are now. Approximately one American in five (21 percent) thinks that relations will improve in the years ahead, while a somewhat smaller proportion (14 percent) expects them to decline. One group—Americans 18 to 29 years of age—is significantly more optimistic about the future than the nation as a whole; 31 percent of the younger generation look for improvement in future years.

Bilateral Issues

Japanese Rearmament

We noted earlier that a majority of Americans are willing to see current U.S. troop levels in Japan maintained or increased, and 50 percent of Americans would support U.S. military intervention should Japan be attacked by either the Soviet Union or the People's Republic of China. We asked our sample their views about a related issue, Japanese rearmament.

> *Under the provisions of the Japanese constitution approved by the American military occupation after World War II, Japan can have only limited military forces for defense. Some Americans believe that Japan should contribute more toward its own defense, and not continue to depend so heavily on the United States. Other Americans feel that a rearmed Japan might become a threat to the security of America or our allies. How do you, yourself, feel about this—do you think Japan should build up a larger military force for defense, or not?*

Should build larger military force	46%
Should not	37
Don't know	17

Americans are quite ambivalent toward Japanese rearmament. A plurality favors a more heavily armed Japan, but those who are opposed are also substantial in number. The college-educated are more in favor of a rearmed Japan than any other group of Americans: 60 percent say yes, and only 30 percent say no.

The fact that the largest bloc of Americans supports rearmament is further evidence of how attitudes have changed since the end of World War II. But the divided response to this question suggests that memories do remain; the notion of a strongly armed Japan is a source of uncertainty and concern for many Americans. Differences among various age groups are sharp. While 51 percent of those 18 to 29 years of age favor Japan's building a larger military force, such backing drops off marginally among those 30 to

49 and 50 to 64 years of age, and then plummets to 30 percent in favor and 46 percent opposed among Americans 65 or older.

Cause of Trade Imbalance

We noted earlier that most Americans are aware of the current imbalance in trade between the United States and Japan: 70 percent know that the United States currently buys more from Japan than it sells to her, while only 5 percent believe the opposite. What do Americans think is behind Japanese dominance of trade between the two countries?

> *Do you think Japanese companies have been so successful in selling their products in the United States because Japanese companies are very efficient and thus able to produce high quality goods at relatively low cost, or is it because Japanese wages are lower than American, or is it because Japanese companies work closely with the Japanese government and thus keep their prices down through government subsidies?*

Japanese companies are more efficient.	16%
Japanese wages are lower.	57
Japanese companies are subsidized.	14
Don't know	13

The notion of "Japan, Inc."—the idea of a highly modernized Japanese industrial plant and close collusion between the Japanese government and the major exporting companies—does not seem to have registered strongly on Americans as a whole. By clustering around the idea of lower wages as the principal reason for Japanese success in business, Americans may be revealing the staying power of the stereotype of Asian cheap "coolie" labor. Even many Americans with a college education are susceptible to this stereotype: 46 percent of them ascribe Japanese business success to low wages.

Basis for Product Choice

In light of the substantial penetration of the American market by Japanese consumer goods, we tried to get a sense of how Americans choose between competing products.

> *Suppose you are shopping and comparing between similar products made in the United States and Japan. Listed on this card are four possible reasons why you might pick one product to purchase over another. Please pick the most important and the next most important reasons that you usually consider.*

Prefer the product because it's made in the United States if it's just as good.	57%
Prefer the product because it's made in Japan if it's just as good.	5
Prefer the product that costs less if it's just as good no matter where it's made.	46
Prefer the better product regardless of where it is made, even if it costs more.	50
Don't know.	3

In terms of "buy American" versus "buy Japanese," it is clear that the "buy American" sentiment dominates overwhelmingly, running as high as 74 percent among those aged 50 to 64. On the other hand, there is a narrow split between those who opt for the better deal on price (mentioned by 46 percent) and those who choose on the basis of quality, even if it means paying more (mentioned by 50 percent). Since there are multiple responses to this question, it is not possible to determine the tradeoffs made by each individual. What *is* clear is that individuals differentiate far more sharply on the basis of where a product is made than according to price versus quality.

Impact of Trade Imbalance

The trade imbalance between the United States and Japan does concern many Americans, judging from responses to the following question.

To what extent do you feel that the products imported from Japan have contributed to our problem of unemployment and lack of job opportunities in the United States? Would you say they have contributed a great deal, some, very little, or not at all?

Great deal	42%
Some	36
Very little	11
None at all	4
Don't know	7

More than three Americans in four (78 percent) say that Japanese imports have made at least some contribution to unemployment in the United States. The very nature of this question and the sensitive subject it addresses probably make it easy for many respondents to pick either the "great deal" or "some" option: the question itself may implant the idea that Japanese exports contribute to unemployment here. Still, we think it would be a mistake to dismiss these responses out of hand and to ignore the protectionists and even latent anti-Japanese sentiment they may encompass.

Building Japanese Plants Here

That this may be the case is suggested by responses to another economic question posed in our survey.

> *Some Japanese companies want to build factories in the United States in which Americans would be employed to produce Japanese products. Do you think the U.S. should try to make it easy for such companies to produce Japanese products, make it hard for such companies to produce Japanese products, or doesn't this make much difference to you?*

Should make it easy	32%
Should make it difficult	37
Makes no difference to me	21
Don't know	10

Particularly significant, perhaps even startling, in these responses is that opposition to making it easy for Japanese companies to build factories in the United States draws a plurality even when it is made clear that the employees will be American. Those most opposed include Midwesterners, traditionally more conservative in their foreign policy views, and those 65 and over, who are consistently less favorable toward the Japanese. Those most inclined to make plant construction easy include men, political independents, and the college-educated. Yet in no case does sentiment for "making it easy" approach majority proportions; the highest figure is 39 percent, among men.

Surely one can argue that the seeds of American protectionism are there.

Notes

1. See page 64, below, for specific data concerning China.
2. See William Watts and Lloyd A. Free, *State of the Nation III* (Lexington, Mass.: Lexington Books, D.C. Heath, 1978), pp. 10-11, 158-160, 177-178.
3. See William Watts and Lloyd A. Free, *State of the Nation III* (Lexington, Mass.: Lexington Books, D.C. Heath, 1978), pp. 127-129.

3 A Look to the Future

As Japanese and Americans look at each other, there are some intangible but fundamental differences in approach. It is as if a long and powerful telescope were stretched across the Pacific Ocean, with the Japanese looking through the small end, seeing the United States enormously magnified, with all our strengths and weaknesses looming even larger than they do for Americans. In its concentrated efforts to modernize and catch up with the West after centuries of isolation, Japan chose the United States as its model in many fields. The American military occupation and the continuing American presence in Japan—not only of troops and bases, but also of businessmen, academics, tourists, and popular culture, including American movies, baseball, fast-food restaurants, blue jeans, television programs, and magazines—have brought our thought and lifestyles to virtually every Japanese household. Several thousand American books are translated into Japanese each year. In 1977 some 750,000 Japanese visited the United States, far the most popular trip for Japanese tourists. In short, the Japanese feel they know us well and feel more comfortable with us than with almost any other foreign country.

The effect of all this on the Japanese has been to produce a kind of love-hate relationship. In spite of the many ties of friendship and familiarity, there is also much antipathy, particularly among intellectuals, writers, and journalists, some of whom are among the most severe critics of the United States anywhere in the whole world. These writers deplore the "materialistic" or "militaristic" influence American culture has had on Japan, or they fear that the distinctive Japanese culture is being undermined by foreign influence. Many of these critics are, of course, Marxists, but many are not, and they are by no means limited to followers of the opposition communist or socialist parties. Their views, although broadly disseminated by the mass media in Japan, are seldom translated into English. This makes it quite possible for Americans in Japan to be oblivious to this strong counterpoint theme in Japanese attitudes toward the United States and its influence.

Americans, looking through the wide end of the telescope, if they look at all, tend to see something much smaller and less significant than the reality. Because of the difficulty of learning Japanese—particularly written Japanese, which requires memorizing a minimum of 1850 Chinese characters—few Americans can communicate effectively with the Japanese or appreciate the richness and diversity of Japanese culture. Only about 25 Japanese books are translated into English each year. Of the several dozen American correspondents in Tokyo, at best a handful can speak Japanese (virtually all the 40-odd Japanese correspondents in Washington can speak passable English). For every student in the United States studying Japanese in the early 1970s, there were 10 studying Russian and 100 studying French. Less than 1 percent of American college students receive even the most superficial exposure to Japanese history and culture. The United States government now has a well-trained corps of Japan specialists, but it remains to be seen how many will reach senior policy-making positions. Japan enters sporadically into the consciousness of most Americans, and then only in small fragments of reality.

In this imbalanced relationship, the Japanese are uneasy about their dependence on the United States and are seeking ways to reaffirm their "separateness" even as they become increasingly dependent on the international community. The pendulum—which swung toward opening up the nation to foreign influences in the 1853-1880 period, again in the 1920s, and yet again in the post-World War II period—is swinging back toward a closing of the door, as in the 1880s and 1930s. The internal debate that has underlaid all Japanese foreign policy decisions for the past century pits the "open-country" (*kaikoku*) advocates against the "closed-country" (*sakoku*) advocates. Today, the open-country faction would liberalize trade even further, would welcome even greater interdependence with the world economy, and would rest secure that Japanese culture is strong enough to remain vital and true to itself in the face of even more foreign involvement in Japan. The more conservative and traditional closed-country faction, on the other hand, believes Japan must protect its agricultural base in case it finds itself isolated in the world. Thus this faction favors trade restrictions, limits on foreign investment, and a return to a more nationalistic outlook in foreign affairs.

As this century-old debate proceeds in Japan, Americans are reassessing their own views of Asia in general and of Japan in particular. As the survey results in the preceding section show clearly, the disastrous war in Vietnam has not discouraged most Americans from seeking close and continuing ties with Japan, our major ally in the Pacific. In fact, the old stereotypes of the Japanese, born at the turn of the century and hardened during World War II, are giving way dramatically to a far more accurate and favorable picture—one that may come as something of a surprise to the Japanese themselves. While our European allies still capture more sympathy and support than Japan among Americans, it is significant that Japan has come to hold a special place in the public mind and that the most supportive Americans are among the younger and better-educated groups.

What does this mean for the future of the United States-Japan relationship? The generally positive American perceptions provide a reassuring and yet cautionary backdrop against which negotiators can try to resolve current economic strains and differences. In particular, if present trading trends continue, pressures for protectionist policies already implicit in some of our findings surely will grow. While they can be offset partially by the basically favorable attitudes that seem to have taken strong root in the public mind, only the most shortsighted observer would deny that such pressures could lead to anti-Japanese legislative or executive actions and a sharply negative turn in American attitudes.

When one examines the currents of opinion in each country, there is a disturbing asymmetry: just when Americans are becoming aware of the beneficial importance of Japan to the United States, many Japanese seem to be losing confidence in the American ability to provide leadership in the world. Increasingly, Japanese leaders are willing to say in public what they have been thinking privately for several years: the United States appears to be losing its nerve, its readiness to assert its power, its willingness to take realistic measures to support the dollar and put its economic house in order, its interest in Asia, and its ability to lead on the economic, political, and security fronts.

These are incipient trends, and it is by no means too late to reverse those that are negative. But it will take enlightened leadership in the public and private sectors on both sides as well as continuing public education. If the United States and Japan can devise new ways to create more balanced trading patterns and to steer their economies along complementary rather than competitive courses, if they can avoid sudden, startling "shocks" and strengthen their sense of partnership, then the open-country advocates in Japan will win their internal debate, with benefits for their own country and for the world, and the isolationist and protectionist elements in America will be held in check. If, on the other hand, the alliance appears in Japan to create more risks than security, more uncertainty on the economic front than dependability, more encroachment than enrichment, then the closed-country advocates in Japan could gain a greater hearing for their demands to return to nationalistic isolationism which would benefit neither the world nor Japan. And we have little doubt that Americans also could turn away from their current positive outlook if the relationship comes to be perceived as one-sided, with the American consumer, laborer, and businessman on the losing side of the bargain.

The road ahead will not be smooth. Rarely in history has there been an alliance of two dissimilar great powers on the scale and depth of the United States-Japan partnership. Whether one looks at the huge amount of trade, the security treaty, or the other exchanges that have bound us together across the Pacific, the alliance is a unique phenomenon that will affect the course of world history in profound ways. There is no precedent in history for one great power (in the economic sphere) to rely for its security on another great power thousands of miles away.

Can great nations of East and West meet in conditions of equality to achieve shared goals? The Soviet Union and the People's Republic of China, so far at least, have not been able to bridge the gap, despite their professed allegiance to a common political philosophy. Is it possible for a continental power such as the United States, with its heritage of isolationism and manifest destiny, to take seriously and to learn from a small, island nation with its own isolationist past, inhabited by an industrious, sensitive, and culturally distinct people?

If Japan and the United States can devise ways to overcome their differences and move forward together to create a peaceful and economically thriving zone in the Pacific Basin, then the potential for progress is enormous. If they fail in this experiment and lapse once again into discord and strife, the negative impact will be global in scope with ramifications one shudders to contemplate.

There are constructive steps—formal and informal, official and unofficial, public and private—that both nations can take now to alleviate strains and build a brighter future. If explained properly to the American people and carried forward in a spirit of cooperation and mutual respect, most of these steps should find public support in this country and help alleviate those doubts that many Americans hold about certain Japanese activities.

In the economic arena, a number of steps are possible.

(1) The United States can do more to assist Japan to overcome its deep anxieties about the sources of markets, supplies, and raw materials, especially energy, with benefits not only for Japan but also for itself. Japan can undertake responsible and responsive measures in turn.

The two countries can enter into long-term agreements on food and grain supplies that will benefit American farmers as well as Japanese consumers. The United States can stockpile food supplies to ensure a dependable source of supplies for Japan. Japan, relieved of its insecurity, can lift its restrictive trade measures and allow American agricultural products to enter its markets freely. A climate of confidence must prevail in order for conservative Japanese politicians to move in this direction, but firm leadership on both sides of the Pacific could cause it to happen.

The Japanese government can do more in the short term to prevent flooding the American market. Japan must understand that no nation will tolerate a systematic exploitation of its markets over the long haul if the cost is widescale domestic unemployment. Japan has already shown restraint in this regard, but it must do more. Tariff and export policies should be reviewed by the Japanese and United States governments to encourage greater economic interchange and investment opportunities.

The U.S. government can do more to help right the United States-Japan trade imbalance, first by curbing inflation and promoting productivity at home. It should firmly insist that Japan lower remaining trade restrictions and at the same time commit itself to the principle of free trade by offering tax incentives to American firms which adapt productive facilities to international markets. The U.S. government can provide means of financing more attractive to American export industries through the Export-Import Bank (especially for our food and fiber products) and should upgrade the quality of our commercial representatives in Japan. In these ways, the United States can recognize—as other advanced nations did long ago—how vital our international trade is to our overall economic well-being.

In addition, the private sectors in both Japan and the United States, which are responsible in the main for the unprecedented affluence in each country, should develop policies and agreements that will promote freer competition, more direct investment, and the establishment of joint ventures beneficial to both sides. The building of plants in the United States to assemble Japanese products, and vice versa, would help ease unemployment pressures and further disruption of the dollar-yen balance.

To be sure, this is an unusually complicated and tricky area, with not only Japanese and American interests at stake but also the interests of other nations competitive in the same production line. But just as the Boeing Company has entered into agreements with Italian companies for design and production cooperation in the new generation of Boeing aircraft, so U.S. and Japanese companies can develop mutually beneficial, cooperative arrangements.

The United States should make an exception for Japan in the case of plutonium, approving the construction of the reprocessing plant at Tokaimura for use in the fast-breeder reactor. No nation will be more cautious than Japan in safeguarding the fuel and technology. United States refusal to provide Japan with enriched uranium would not be effective, since Japan would simply obtain it elsewhere. Meanwhile the alliance would be weakened, and pressure within Japan to arm itself with nuclear weapons might well be increased. Efforts to curb the spread of nuclear arms should be carried out by both nations in multilateral forums.

(2) On the diplomatic front, both the United States and Japan should consult more closely. With respect to the U.S. plan to withdraw ground forces from South Korea, Japanese support and cooperation should be sought at every step. Both the United States and Japan should work together to establish a common vision for the long-term future of the Korean peninsula and to negotiate with the People's Republic of China, the Soviet Union, and North and South Korea to lessen the danger of war and provide stability in that potentially explosive arena.

With respect to Southeast Asia, the United States and Japan should cooperate in trade and economic aid, and Japan should bear some part of the burden for U.S. efforts to provide security for the region. Neither government should seek as a policy to predominate in the region.

The United States should support more strongly Japan's efforts to attain a permanent seat on the United Nations Security Council and welcome other Japanese initiatives in international forums.

(3) On the security front, in its own self-interest Japan must do more to relieve the United States of the cost of maintaining troops and bases in Japan and to strengthen Japanese self-defense forces to the point where Japan could defend itself from conventional attack. Japan should move in these directions of its own volition, rather than under prodding from Washington. Japanese initiatives in this direction will help to deflect protectionist sentiment in Congress.

(4) In their unofficial bilateral relations, each nation must do more to educate and inform important segments of the public about the other nation.

American exporters must learn to meet the requirements of the Japanese market if the two-way trade is to thrive, a skill that thus far has eluded a higher proportion of our businessmen. More intensive links should be developed between business leadership groups in Japan and the United States, to promote such understanding.

The Japanese must overcome their sense of separateness by expanding the teaching of English, inviting more outside teachers to their great universities, and opening up their nation much as the United States had opened up its own to international influences. American educators, particularly at the secondary levels, should drop the ethnocentric view that world history centers about Europe and the United States and should teach more about the great civilizations of Asia.

Americans must do far more in the area of education and cultural exchange and strengthening the study of Japanese language and culture in schools and colleges. The American mass media should give greater emphasis to sophisticated, accurate reporting on Japan and to conveying a true picture of Japan to the American public.

(5) To educate and inform citizens in both Japan and the United States about the importance of their relationship and the need for both powers to improve understanding and communication with the other Pacific nations, a new Council of the Pacific might be organized. Comprised of private citizens in the Pacific nations, its purpose would be to exchange ideas and information with the goal of promoting peace, prosperity, and mutual understanding throughout the Pacific basin. Through discussion groups, seminars, publications, and other forums, members would be invited to design new ways to cooperate in economic development, cultural exchanges, and education about each other. One purpose of the new body would be to bring home to the American people and their leaders the fact that we are, and will increasingly be, a Pacific nation. In 1977, for the first time in history, our trade with Asian nations exceeded our trade with Europe, and the trend is likely to continue.

The United States-Japan relationship should and can be the most important bilateral relationship for each country in the coming decades. As we have seen, the shape of American public opinion is, in large measure, congruent with this concept. Leaders in and out of government in both countries are faced with an enormous challenge and opportunity to devise policies that will enhance our mutual bonds. The few steps outlined here represent only a beginning. The course and nature of relations between the United States and Japan will be among the principal factors in determining the history of this planet through the end of this century and beyond.

Part II:
Korea

4 Policy Setting

"Koreagate"

On February 26, 1978 a composed and dapper Korean businessman arrived at National Airport in Washington, D.C., where he was met by a crowd of reporters. The nation learned of his arrival on the evening news. Tongsun Park, the central figure in a sensational, influence-buying scandal on Capitol Hill, had come to testify before congressional committees and in court on his role in passing money to members of Congress.

Beginning in the autumn of 1976, the ramifications of what came to be called "Koreagate" dominated reporting on Korea in the American press. Stories ranged from the financial operations of Reverend Sun Myung Moon's Unification Church and Korean CIA activities in the United States to allegations that President Park Chung-hee himself in 1970 had ordered the massive campaign to win support for South Korea from senators and representatives through lavish entertainment and sizable gifts of cash. Congressional investigators sought the testimony of the former Korean ambassador in Washington, Kim Dong Jo, who was accused of direct involvement in the giving of money to members of Congress. Lengthy investigations of the various allegations by the Justice Department and by several congressional committees resulted in the indictment of two former congressmen for receiving bribes: Richard T. Hanna (D., Calif.) and Otto E. Passman (D., La.). Tongsun Park and another Korean businessman were also indicted.

The "Koreagate" revelations strained relations between the United States and South Korea. Americans resented the Korean attempt to buy influence in Congress. Koreans were irritated by demands that their ambassador be compelled to submit to interrogation by foreign authorities, and they were outraged when a former American ambassador in Seoul indicated that U.S. agents had bugged President Park Chung-hee's executive mansion in the 1960s.

By the summer of 1978 the various investigations into possible illegal or unethical actions by Koreans and members of Congress seemed to be winding down. Tongsun Park's testimony proved anti-climactic, confirming facts previously known but providing little new information. The wrongdoing uncovered was considerably less extensive than some early speculation had forecast. Although the investigation was necessary and constituted a salutary warning against improper relations between members of Congress and foreign nationals, the almost exclusive attention given by the media for the better part of two years to this single aspect of U.S. relations with South Korea was unfortunate. More important issues crying out for public attention and debate have been slighted.

Among such issues were the wisdom of President Carter's decision to withdraw U.S. ground forces from South Korea by 1982, which had been questioned in Congress and elsewhere, and the appropriate action to take on administration proposals for substantial grants and loans to increase and modernize the weapons of the South Korean armed forces. The long-term implications of South Korea's rapid economic growth, its authoritarian political system, and its increasing ability to produce nuclear weapons all merited attention from Americans. North Korean proposals for direct talks with the United States spotlighted the need for a U.S. diplomatic strategy to complement the U.S. troop withdrawal plan. Searching discussion of these matters, basic to the prospects for long-term peace and stability in East Asia but long preempted by "Koreagate," is overdue.

Korea and the Big Powers

Throughout its history Korea has been subject to invasion by neighboring peoples. The Chinese invaded and controlled parts of Korea before it became a unified state in the seventh century. Later, nomadic tribes harassed its borders from Manchuria, sometimes penetrating deeply. In 1259 the Korean ruler capitulated to the Mongols, who controlled the country for the next century. Korea became a tributary state of the Ming dynasty in China (1368-1644) and highly receptive to Chinese culture, although not actually ruled by the Chinese. Japanese invaders devasted the peninsula in the sixteenth century, and in the seventeenth century the Koreans were subjugated by the Manchus before the Manchus went on to conquer China. By the nineteenth century, Russia had appeared on the scene, a new rival for power over Korea. But by defeating China in 1894-1895 and Russia in 1904-1905, the Japanese won the contest and in 1910 made Korea a Japanese colony.

The Koreans were never assimilated by their conquerors. Their traditional political system, art, literature, and religion were strongly influenced by China, but Koreans retained their own distinctive language, customs, and cultural identity. After the Manchu conquest they deliberately isolated their country from outside contacts, except with China and to a very limited extent with Japan. In ethnic terms they are today one of the most homogeneous nations.

Koreans look back with bitterness on their 35 years as colonial subjects of Japan. Although the country was developed economically, the benefits went mostly to the Japanese, who owned nearly 90 percent of the industry as well as large amounts of land. Under the Japanese the number of tenant farmers increased and average rice consumption declined. The Japanese occupied the great majority of senior and middle-level positions in the bureaucracy and constituted over 85 percent of the police. Moreover, the Japanese tried to eradicate the cultural identity of the Koreans. Prime Minister Hara Kei declared in 1919, "We will not, however, waver in our determination to Japanize the Korean people, for we believe that our intention is right and just and that in Japanizing them we are promoting their welfare." The Japanese forbade the use of the Korean language in schools and banned Korean publications and the study of Korean history. They forced Koreans to adopt Japanese surnames and introduced Shintoism into the schools.

Japanese repression stimulated Korean nationalism. On March 1, 1919 a group of Korean leaders in Seoul, influenced by President Woodrow Wilson's statements on the self-determination of peoples, proclaimed Korea's independence. The nationwide demonstrations that followed were harshly suppressed by Japanese security forces, who killed, injured, or arrested thousands of Koreans. Korean exile groups responded to the abortive movement for independence within Korea by intensifying their nationalist activities. A Korean provisional government was formed in Shanghai, naming Syngman Rhee, then residing in the United States, as president. Throughout the 1920s and 1930s Korean exiles in China, the United States, and the Soviet Union continued anti-Japanese activities, but intrafactional conflict limited their effectiveness. Korean guerrillas in Manchuria made occasional forays into northern Korea until they were wiped out or driven into Soviet territory by Japanese forces occupying Manchuria after 1931.

During World War II leaders of the United States, Great Britain, and China agreed to strip Japan of its overseas territories. They declared at Cairo on December 1, 1943 that "in due course Korea shall become free and independent." The Cairo Declaration was reaffirmed at the Potsdam Conference of July 1945 and subsequently accepted by the Soviet Union.

For the purpose of receiving the surrender of Japanese forces on the Korean peninsula, Washington and Moscow agreed that Soviet troops would stay north of the 38th parallel and U.S. forces would occupy the area south of that line. That division, intended as a temporary military measure, has resisted all attempts at unification of the Korean people. A U.S.-Soviet proposal in December 1945 to create a trusteeship over a unified Korea for a period of up to five years failed when it was vehemently opposed by all political groups in Korea except the communists. A 1947 resolution of the UN General Assembly providing for elections throughout Korea to form a single government also failed to break the deadlock: the Soviets refused to permit UN-supervised elections in territory under their occupation. As a result, elections were held in the southern part of Korea only, leading to the formation of a government in Seoul which on August 15, 1948 proclaimed the establishment of the Republic of Korea and was recognized by the United Nations as the only legitimate government on the peninsula. Less than a month later, the establishment of the Democratic People's Republic of Korea was announced in Pyongyang.

In June 1950, emboldened by the withdrawal of all U.S. forces from Korea and a declaration excluding Korea from the U.S. defense perimeter in the western Pacific, Kim Il-sung launched his attempt to unify Korea by force, taking advantage of North Korea's superiority in arms over South Korea. The United Nations Security Council condemned North Korea as an aggressor and authorized the creation of a United Nations Command to help South Korea resist the invasion. The United Nations Command, composed of U.S. and South Korean troops and small contingents sent by several other UN members, drove the North Koreans back across the 38th parallel and then, in its turn, sought to unify Korea by force by extending its occupation to the Yalu River, bordering China. Chinese intervention pushed UN forces out of North Korea, and the war then settled into an indecisive struggle.

An armistice was finally agreed to in July 1953. It provided for a military demarcation line between the two sides running generally along the 38th parallel. The armistice agreement also created a demilitarized zone 2½ miles wide on either side of the military demarcation line; a military armistice commission to supervise maintenance of the armistice, composed of representatives of the UN Command, North Korea, and the People's Republic of China (South Korea refused to sign the armistice agreement); and a Neutral Nations Supervisory Commission made up of representatives from Sweden, Switzerland, Poland, and Czechoslovakia to watch for and investigate violations of the agreement. The United States designates the United Nations Commander, as provided by a UN resolution, which places on the U.S. government special responsibility for maintaining the armistice. Efforts to replace the armistice agreement with a political settlement have failed, leaving the two Koreas to confront each other for over a quarter of a century in an uneasy truce.

The destruction, death, and suffering caused by the Korean war had a profound impact on the two Koreas. Fear of war and determination to prevent its recurrence were widespread. Leaders on both sides recognized that their governments owed their survival to foreign intervention. Yet it was foreign intervention that had divided Korea in the first place and had made the war far more destructive than if it had been an exclusively Korean affair. Consequently, both North and South Koreans had ambivalent attitudes toward their big power protectors. They needed their help in reconstructing the economies and equipping the armed forces. They also relied on them in extremity to guarantee the survival of their political systems. But this heavy dependence on foreign nations was frustrating and went against the grain of Korean nationalism.

South Koreans felt that they were in a more precarious situation than North Koreans, for their big power protector was located 6000 miles away. Americans might or might not come to their aid again if they were attacked by North Korea. The People's Republic of China and the Soviet Union, on the other hand, had a strong and enduring interest in preserving the communist buffer state on their borders. This geopolitical asymmetry caused South Koreans to want U.S. forces to remain on their territory and led them to discount the significance of the withdrawal of Chinese forces in 1958 from North Korea across the Yalu River to positions in Manchuria from which they could return quickly if needed.

The Korean war also had a profound impact on American policy. It resulted in a rapid buildup in U.S. forces and a major strengthening of NATO, for the attack in Korea appeared to demonstrate that the Sino-Soviet bloc would strike at any weakness in defense of the noncommunist world. It brought about a reversal of President Truman's hands-off policy toward Taiwan, leading to increased U.S. involvement with Taiwan and adoption of a policy of containment toward the People's Republic of China. It stimulated Japan's economic recovery and accelerated the signing of a peace treaty with Japan, the beginning of Japanese rearmament, and the conclusion of a security treaty between the United States and Japan. And with respect to Korea, it brought about the reintroduction of U.S. forces there, a security treaty between the United States and the Republic of Korea, and large-scale programs of U.S. economic and military assistance which, by 1977, amounted to $5.2 billion and $7 billion, respectively.

Both the Soviet Union and the People's Republic of China helped rebuild North Korea's economy and reequip its armed forces, although the Soviets were more important suppliers than the Chinese, especially of weapons. In 1961 North Korea signed defense treaties with both the Soviet Union and China. When the Sino-Soviet dispute heated up in the early 1960s, North Korean leader Kim Il-sung, after attempting for a short time to remain neutral, leaned toward China. As a result, the Soviets cut off economic and military aid entirely for several years. They resumed aid in the mid-1960s, and Pyongyang's relations with Peking cooled during the Cultural Revolution in China. In 1970 Chou En-lai visited Pyongyang to restore friendly relations. Since that time, North Korea has had somewhat better relations with China than with the Soviet Union. In the spring of 1975, as South Vietnam was collapsing, Kim Il-sung traveled to Peking, where he obtained explicit public recognition of his government as the "sole legal sovereign state of the Korean nation" and made belligerent threats against South Korea. But Chinese public statements were significantly more restrained than Kim's, and the Russians rebuffed his request to stop in Moscow on his trip.

Even before the Soviets had pressured North Korea by cutting off military and economic aid, Kim had adopted a policy of reducing as rapidly as possible North Korea's dependence on the Soviet Union and mainland China. In public speeches he lashed out at the "big-power chauvinism" displayed by the big communist nations, and he channeled extensive resources into building up North Korea's own heavy industry and weapons production capability. In the early 1970s he tried, not very successfully, to diversify North Korea's foreign trade. Although North Korea remains dependent on the Soviet Union and China for some critical items, especially petroleum products and advanced weapons, the Sino-Soviet dispute allows North Korea to play off one against the other and to manipulate both into backing the main lines of its policy.

Japan's relations with the two Koreas have been particularly sensitive because of Korean resentment at the way they were treated by the Japanese during the colonial period. Negotiations between South Korea and Japan, begun in 1951 and strongly encouraged by the United States, were broken off repeatedly. Relations were not established until 1965, over bitter protests from Korean students and other opponents of the government. In the treaty establishing diplomatic relations, Japan recognized the Republic of Korea as "the only lawful government in Korea, as specified in the resolution of the United Nations." Nonetheless, it has engaged in trade and unofficial contacts with North Korea despite South Korean objections.

Recurring strains in relations between Japan and South Korea have not prevented the two countries from forging close bonds. Japan has become South Korea's principal supplier of foreign capital and technology. In 1969 Prime Minister Eisaku Sato declared, in a communiqué issued jointly with President Nixon, that the security of South Korea was essential to the security of Japan. Subsequent Japanese governments have continued to stress the importance to Japan of peace and stability in Korea.

Of the four big powers concerned with Korea, the United States has been the most intimately involved. Since 1958, when Chinese troops withdrew, it has been the only outside power with military forces stationed on the Korean peninsula. Relations with North Korea have been confined almost exclusively to the usually ritualistic Military Armistice Commission meetings between American and North Korean commanders at Panmunjom in the DMZ, or hostile clashes, as when the North Koreans captured the electronic surveillance ship *Pueblo* in 1968, shot down an EC-121 aircraft in 1969, or killed two American officers with axes in the DMZ in 1976. Few Americans have been permitted to visit North Korea. Since 1974 Kim Il-sung has called for direct negotiations between Pyongyang and Washington on a peace treaty and on the withdrawal of U.S. forces from Korea, bypassing the South Korean government. The U.S. government has refused, however, to negotiate with North Korea without the participation of South Korea.

U.S. relations with South Korea have been close but not always smooth. Rapid economic growth in South Korea during the latter half of the 1960s and improvements in the South Korean armed forces, which sent two divisions to fight in Vietnam during this period, convinced President Nixon that the United States could safely withdraw from South Korea in 1971 one of the two combat divisions maintained there. The South Korean government at first objected strongly, but eventually acquiesced in exchange for the United States' promise to provide a large amount of equipment to modernize South Korean forces. Delay in completing this program created skepticism among South Koreans that the military equipment proposed by the Carter administration as compensation for the withdrawal of the remaining U.S. ground forces would be provided as scheduled.

Although the commitment of the United States to the defense of South Korea remains the primary link between the two countries, the economic relationship is growing rapidly in importance as South Korea's economy expands. Of South Korea's $21 billion foreign trade in 1977, 27 percent was with the United States. Already South Korea has become the fourteenth largest trading partner of the United States, buying nearly $1 billion in agricultural commodities each year in addition to purchasing civilian aircraft, military equipment, and other high-technology products. American private firms have invested some $950 million in loans and equity in South Korea.

Evolution of the Two Koreas

Each of the Koreas patterned its political and economic system in general after that of its superpower patron, but with extensive modifications. Thus, the Republic of Korea is a constitutional democracy in form, but during most of its history authoritarian rulers have abridged the political and civil rights of the people to a greater or lesser degree. Economically, South Korea basically follows the tenets of free enterprise but with more extensive government involvement through planning and coordination in economic affairs than is practiced in the United States.

North Korea, although it has a political and economic system similar in structure to that of the Soviet Union, regiments its people much more sternly than either the Soviet Union or China. The wife of a Soviet journalist stationed in Peking exclaimed to her husband on returning to mainland China from a visit to Pyongyang, "How good it feels to be back in a free country!" The adulation of Kim Il-sung has been institutionalized in North

Korea at a level of intensity rarely seen elsewhere, exceeded perhaps only by the worship of Mao's thoughts during the most frenetic stage of the Cultural Revolution in China.

South Korea

Political history in South Korea can be divided into two principal periods: the presidency of Syngman Rhee from 1948 to 1960 and the rule of Park Chung-hee, first as the senior military figure following the coup of May 1961 and then as president from 1963 to the present. The two periods were separated by a short interregnum during which Chang Myon governed as prime minister.

The Rule of Syngman Rhee. Syngman Rhee was the best known leader of the Korean independence movement abroad when, at 70 years of age, he returned to Korea in 1945 from many years of exile in the United States. A fervent patriot and astute political tactician, he was elected President of the Republic of Korea in 1948 by an overwhelming majority of the National Assembly. When the North Koreans attacked in 1950, Rhee rallied his people to resist and proved an able war leader. But he was a difficult ally and ill qualified to direct the economic recovery of South Korea after the war or to preside over the introduction of a system of democracy into Korea.

Having just emerged from the grip of Japanese colonialism, the Korean people had no experience in governing themselves. Although Rhee was committed in a formal sense to the establishment of a democratic system in Korea and did, in fact, allow some opposition activity and criticism of the government by the press, he was determined to maintain control firmly in his own hands. He resorted to crude intimidation of opponents and countenanced widespread corruption. Moreover, despite a large inflow of foreign aid that helped repair the ravages of war, his government showed little interest in economic development. Opposition to corruption and to the use of the police to keep Rhee's Liberal Party in power increased to the point where student demonstrations against fraudulent elections in 1960 forced Rhee's resignation.

Interregnum and Coup. The Chang Myon interregnum that followed, which abolished the presidential system and replaced it with a parliamentary system, was the freest period in South Korea's political history. Newpapers proliferated, politicians scrambled for position, and political demonstrators marched daily through the streets of Seoul. Within the National Assembly the Liberal Party dissolved: its members forsook it for Prime Minister Chang's Democratic Party, which promptly split into rival factions, more concerned with securing cabinet positions for their members than in passing legislation. The fierce competition for appointments resulted in an average tenure in office of two months for cabinet officers under the Chang government, as compared to seven months under Rhee.

Under such circumstances, the adoption and execution of effective policies was impossible. Industrial production declined, unemployment increased, and prices rose rapidly. Dissatisfaction mounted, especially within the armed forces, and they brought down the Chang government by a military coup in May 1961 after only nine months in office. The ineffectiveness of the Chang government and the self-serving behavior of politicians further discredited party politics in the eyes of many Koreans—already disillusioned by politics under Syngman Rhee—and made them receptive to the pledges of the military leaders to bring order and progress to the nation.

The Rule of Park Chung-hee. The military coup had been organized and planned largely by a group of young colonels, who moved swiftly to consolidate their power. They declared martial law, dissolved all political organizations and banned political activity, established censorship over the press, abolished usurious debts owed by farmers and fishermen, established the Korean Central Intelligence Agency (KCIA), began a purge of senior military officers for corruption or for opposing the coup, and fired a large number of government employees on the grounds that they had obtained their jobs through nepotism or bribery.

The senior figure behind the military coup was Major General Park Chung-hee, an uncle by marriage of the most influential of the young colonels, Lieutenant Colonel Kim Chong-pil. The son of a farmer, Park had been a junior officer in the Japanese army and rose to general officer rank in the South Korean army during the Korean war.

In 1962 Park obtained approval through referendum of extensive constitutional amendments, which replaced the parliamentary system of Chang Myon with a system that concentrated power in the hands of the president. Kim Chong-pil set about creating a new party, the Democratic Republic Party (DRP), to support Park and his associates; and in 1963 Park resigned from the army to run for president, defeating by a narrow margin his chief opponent, Yun Po-sun, who had been the figurehead president during the Chang Myon period. Other members of the coup group followed Park's example, doffing their uniforms to become cabinet ministers or to take other important civilian posts in the new administration.

In 1965 President Park, strongly encouraged by the United States, pushed through a treaty normalizing relations with Japan. Vociferous resistance from students, opposition politicians, and intellectuals necessitated the use of troops to maintain public order. In 1967, with South Korea enjoying rapid economic growth as a result of his policies, Park was elected to a second term as president by a comfortable margin. But in 1969 he provoked renewed opposition to his rule, even on the part of some members of his own party, when he rammed through the National Assembly a constitutional amendment authorizing a third term for presidents.

In 1971 Park was elected to a third term but by a narrower margin than in 1967. Likewise, the government party, the DRP, was returned with a majority in the National Assembly but no longer a two-thirds majority. Other developments posed new uncertainties for Park's government. The United States withdrew one of its two combat divisions from South Korea and indicated that further withdrawals could be expected as South Korean forces were strengthened. President Nixon's pursuit of détente with the Soviet Union and his sudden announcement that he would visit Peking disturbed both North and South Korea.

Park took a series of steps to strengthen his ability to cope with domestic and international change. In October 1972 he declared martial law, suspended certain articles of the constitution, and dissolved the National Assembly. Drastic constitutional changes were then adopted through a national referendum in November 1972 while the country was still under martial law; they provided for the election of a National Conference for Unification composed of popularly elected nonparty delegates who would choose a president for a 6-year term. Park was duly elected president by this body for another 6 years in December 1972. The new constitution gave much greater power to the president while weakening the National Assembly and the judiciary. Subsequently, by executive decrees, Park made opposition to the constitution a crime. A number of politicians, students, intellectuals, and Christian ministers who publicly opposed the constitution were arrested, tried, and sentenced to terms in prison. In order to suppress dissent further, KCIA controls over newspapers and student activities were tightened.

Park has sought to justify his stern measures as being necessary to cope with the continuing military and subversive threat from North Korea. His adversaries remain unpersuaded, but KCIA surveillance and decrees forbidding open dissent afford them little room for opposition. The bulk of the population is more concerned with their own material welfare and prospects than with their government's divergence from Western standards of democracy. Rapid economic growth under Park's rule has brought about a general rise in the standard of living and has held out hope for still more gains, justifying in the eyes of many Koreans the methods adopted to achieve these results.

The rate of economic growth in South Korea in recent years has been remarkable. When Park took over the government in 1961, South Korea was among the poorest nations in the world. Per capita GNP was less than

$100. The rate of inflation was high, and domestic savings amounted to less than 5 percent of GNP. The value of imports was 10 times that of exports, and the economy was propped up by heavy infusions of U.S. aid. Many saw South Korea in those days as an economic disaster, a bottomless pit for U.S. aid dollars.

Park instituted sweeping reforms. He devalued the currency, strengthened financial institutions, and gave priority to an expansion of labor-intensive light industry. He aimed at replacing imported consumer goods with domestic products and building up exports of light industrial goods—particularly textiles—manufactured from imported materials. He made economic development a major national goal and inaugurated a series of 5-year plans under which the efforts of government and private enterprise were closely coordinated. After the establishment of diplomatic relations with Japan in 1965, Japanese capital began to flow into South Korea in the form of government loans and private investment. Private investment from the United States and other countries also increased in response to the heightened economic activity in South Korea as well as government measures aimed at attracting investment.

The political stability and economic incentives provided by the Park government created a surge of economic growth rarely seen in developing countries. From 1965 to 1976, South Korea's GNP grew by almost 11 percent annually and per capita GNP by 8.5 percent per year. During this period industrial production was growing at an annual rate close to 25 percent. Agriculture was comparatively neglected in the 1960s, the increase in grain production barely exceeding the rate of population growth. Since 1973, however, as a result of grain price supports and other measures, the annual increase in grain production has averaged close to 7 percent, and the welfare of the rural population has improved considerably.

Today South Korea is in a strong position to continue its rapid economic growth. It no longer relies on U.S. economic aid, instead obtaining foreign loans from banks, private investors, and international financial institutions. Its domestic savings rate reached 21 percent of GNP in 1976, compared to less than 5 percent in the early 1960s. Income is more equitably distributed than in most countries. By 1978 Korean construction companies had won more than $3 billion in overseas contracts, and 90,000 Koreans were at work on construction projects in the Middle East. Invisible earnings in 1977, mainly from the Middle East construction contracts, brought the country's current account into balance. South Korea's low debt-service ratio, which fell to 10 percent in 1977, and its high credit rating made economic officials confident that they could readily achieve a capital inflow of some $2.5 billion annually. This amount is needed to import the $22 billion in modern plant and equipment the current 5-year plan calls for to further develop heavy and technology-intensive industries, such as machine building, steel, electronics, shipbuilding, motor vehicles, petrochemicals, and armaments.

South Korea is troubled by inflation, continued opposition to the government's authoritarian measures, and the prospect of urban unrest arising from rapid social change as millions of people from the countryside crowd into the cities. Nevertheless, a recent U.S. Central Intelligence Agency study predicts an annual South Korean growth rate of 9 to 10 percent during the current 5-year plan ending in 1981, provided that there is no world recession and Korea's principal trading partners do not adopt highly protectionist policies. According to this estimate, South Korea, which recently overtook North Korea in terms of per capita GNP, probably will have an economy three times as large as that of North Korea by the early 1980s.

North Korea

Kim Il-sung, who had been an anti-Japanese guerrilla leader in Manchuria, returned to Korea with Soviet forces in 1945. Although he was only 33 years old at the time and little known to Koreans, firm backing by Soviet occupation forces enabled him to outmaneuver noncommunist and communist rivals. By the time the Democratic People's Republic of Korea was established in Pyongyang in 1948, he was vice-chairman and actual leader of the North Korean Communist party, and he became premier of the new government. Land reform, nationalization of transportation, communications, banking, and basic industries, as well as other actions aimed at creating a full-fledged communist state, had already been carried out under Soviet supervision. Confident that the Communist party under Kim's leadership was firmly in control, Soviet occupation forces withdrew from Korea in December 1948.

Kim Il-sung's leadership did not go unchallenged. Potential rivals existed in three factions inside the party: communists who had been active in Korea prior to 1945, those who had been based in Yenan, China, and Koreans from the Soviet Union, some of whom were Soviet citizens. By the end of the Korean war, Kim had eliminated his chief rival in the domestic faction; later he purged the Yenan and Soviet factions. By the late 1950s he was firmly entrenched as the supreme ruler.

Speeches by leading officials and editorials in the controlled press credit Kim with superhuman wisdom and accomplishments. He has been exalted so far above any other North Korean leader that agreement on a successor to his one-man rule may be difficult. Over the years he has come to rely increasingly on members of his own family and aging comrades who were with him in Manchuria. For several years Kim apparently had been grooming his son, Kim Chung-il, as his successor, but the process came to a sudden halt early in 1978 amid rumors that his son had met with a serious accident. Although Kim Il-sung, who is 66, appears active and healthy, the problem of succession will grow more and more pressing.

Economically, North Korea had an advantage over South Korea in 1945, for it possessed the bulk of Korea's mineral resources and most of the power plants and factories built in Korea by the Japanese. Although much of North Korea's industry was destroyed during the Korean war, it was quickly rebuilt with Soviet and Chinese help. Under a plan giving priority to heavy industry, North Korea industrialized rapidly during the 1950s. By 1963 the contribution of industry to national income had increased to over 60 percent, as compared to only 17 percent in 1946. Industrial expansion was accompanied by the growth of cities and enlargement and improvement of the educational system. Until the mid-1960s North Korea outstripped South Korea in economic growth.

During the 1960s economic growth in North Korea slowed. More investment had to be diverted to agriculture and light industry, which had been neglected. Foreign aid declined, and in the latter half of the 1960s North Korea embarked on a costly program to strengthen the armed forces and to increase domestic production of weapons and other military equipment.

In the early 1970s Kim Il-sung, perhaps impressed by South Korea's foreign trade-based economic takeoff after 1965, began to order large quantities of plants and machinery from Japan and Western Europe. However, the North Koreans lacked the experience and skills which the South Koreans had acquired in large-scale trade and financial transactions with the economies of the noncommunist world. Consequently, they became overcommitted and were unable to cope with the rapid rise in world prices of manufactured goods that followed the quadrupling of oil prices in 1973. They defaulted on their debts and at the end of 1976 still owed some $1.4 billion to Western creditors, about six times their annual, hard-currency exports, plus another $1 billion to communist creditors.

Public statements by Kim Il-sung and other North Korean leaders on the 7-year plan begun in 1978 stress the need to rely on their own human and material resources. The only mention of foreign trade in a speech to the Supreme People's Assembly in December 1977 by the Minister of Foreign Trade referred to the need to produce domestically certain industrial raw materials and machines previously imported. It seems certain that North Korea's inability to compete with South Korea in importing advanced technology will produce a steadily widening technological gap between the two countries.

Military Confrontation and Stalemated Dialogue

Since the end of the Korean war, the two Koreas have faced each other warily across the DMZ, devoting much effort to strengthening their military establishments. South Korea, which has twice the population of North Korea, has maintained more men in uniform but has had fewer planes, warships, tanks, and artillery pieces than North Korea and has lagged behind in military production capability. From 1966 to 1975 the North Koreans allocated between 11 and 17 percent of their GNP to military purposes, compared with 4 to 5 percent in South Korea. Moreover, very early Kim Il-sung began to build heavy industry and an arms production capability, and North Korea now produces heavy artillery, tanks, gunboats, and submarines.

Today, however, South Korea has a heavy industry comparable in most respects to that of North Korea. It has increased the proportion of GNP devoted to military purposes from 5 to 7 percent. Already self-sufficient in the production of small arms, South Korea recently began to manufacture heavy artillery, antiaircraft guns, armored personnel carriers, and naval patrol craft. The U.S. government plans to turn over to the Koreans much of the equipment of the withdrawing U.S. combat division and to provide other weapons by credit sales. Park Chung-hee predicted in January 1978 that by the early 1980s South Korea would be far superior to North Korea in military strength.

South Korea has an ambitious nuclear power program; its first nuclear power reactor came on line in 1978, and five more are under construction or contracted for. The training of South Korean scientists and engineers to operate this program will greatly increase the nation's capability to produce nuclear weapons, because basic nuclear technology can be used for either civilian or military purposes. In 1975 South Korea ordered from France a reprocessing plant that could have produced small amounts of plutonium from the reprocessing of spent fuel from nuclear reactors, but the deal was canceled under pressure from the United States. South Korea has signed the nuclear nonproliferation treaty, pledging not to produce nuclear weapons. Nevertheless, the South Korean government has not ruled out production if, as the result of the withdrawal of U.S. protection, the security of the nation should require it. North Korea has no known plans to build nuclear power plants.

Both the Republic of Korea and the Democratic People's Republic of Korea subscribe in principle to the goal of peaceful unification, but each claims to be the only legitimate government on the peninsula. Until 1971 they did not speak to each other. In that year, influenced by changing international and domestic circumstances, they began a dialogue.

Kim Il-sung's attempts in the late 1960s to assassinate Park Chung-hee and to instigate rebellion in South Korea by infiltrating agents and commando teams had failed. South Korea was outdistancing North Korea in economic growth. The startling announcement in July 1971 that President Nixon would soon visit Peking raised the possibility that the big powers might reach agreements affecting Korea behind the backs of the Koreans themselves. Probably more important than these factors, however, in Kim's decision to begin a dialogue with the Park government was his appraisal of conditions in South Korea and South Korean relations with the United States. Opposition figures in South Korea were calling for negotiations with North Korea on unification. The Nixon administration had withdrawn one of the two U.S. combat divisions in South Korea and had indicated that more U.S. forces would be withdrawn as South Korean forces grew stronger. Kim probably thought that negotiations between Pyongyang and Seoul could be used to strengthen Park's opponents and to accelerate the withdrawal of U.S. forces, whose presence he considered the prime obstacle to the reunification of Korea on his terms.

Park's decision to enter the dialogue seemed more defensive than Kim's. He was disturbed by the withdrawal of American forces as well as by the growing détente between the United States and the two principal supporters of North Korea—the Soviet Union and mainland China. He probably also felt a need to respond to growing demands in South Korea for talks with Pyongyang. South Korea's impressive economic performance since 1965 and Park's election to a third term in April 1971 placed the government in a relatively favorable position to make the unprecedented move.

In the autumn of 1971 Seoul and Pyongyang agreed that the Red Cross societies of the two countries should begin talks aimed at reuniting families separated by the division of Korea. In July 1972 representatives of the two governments announced agreement to seek national unity, transcending ideologies and systems, and to achieve unification peacefully, by Korean efforts alone, without outside interference. They agreed to take measures to prevent military incidents, to install a direct telephone line between Seoul and Pyongyang, to press ahead with the Red Cross talks, to carry out exchanges in various fields, to refrain from defaming each other, and to set up a South-North Coordinating Committee to implement the foregoing steps and to settle the unification problem.

Meetings of representatives of the two Red Cross societies and of members of the South-North Coordinating Committee took place alternately in Seoul and Pyongyang in late 1972 and early 1973 in an atmosphere of hope and excitement. But little progress was made in the two series of talks, and in mid-1973 Pyongyang refused to continue with the meetings of the principal Coordinating Committee or Red Cross representatives in the two capitals. Lower-ranking representatives continued to meet from time to time at Panmunjom, but the talks had reached an impasse. Pyongyang throughout insisted on negotiating broad and basic issues, such as setting up a confederation of the two Koreas or sharply reducing the military forces on each side, while Seoul proposed beginning with less difficult issues, such as exchanges of persons or correspondence between divided families. The two sides mostly talked past each other and made little effort to probe each other's positions in order to reach compromise. The attempted assassination of Park Chung-hee in 1974, in which his wife was killed by a North Korean agent, and the discovery of tunnels under the DMZ dug by North Korea in the early 1970s increased South Korean distrust of North Korean intentions.

Competition for International Status

The involvement of the United States and the Soviet Union in Korea, first as sponsors of rival governments and then as the principal supporters of these governments in the Korean war, turned the question of who should rule Korea into a major, international issue. Each Korean government, aided by its backers, has engaged in a continuing contest to increase international support for its position and to weaken support for its rival.

Much of the contention for international status between the two Koreas has occurred within the United Nations. Here the South Korean government had an initial advantage because the UN had recognized its legitimacy and had condemned North Korea as an aggressor. South Korea was granted observer status in the UN in 1951. During the 1950s the United States and South Korea were more concerned with keeping North Korea out of the world body than with bringing in South Korea. Consequently, they defeated Soviet initiatives in 1957 and 1958 to admit both Koreas to the UN. In addition, resolutions put forward in the UN General Assembly by supporters of North Korea calling for the dissolution of the UN Command and the withdrawal of U.S. forces from Korea were repeatedly defeated.

International support for North Korea gradually increased during the 1960s and early 1970s. In 1973 North Korea won admission to the World Health Organization over the hard-fought opposition of South Korea and its supporters. North Korea was also granted observer status at the UN. South Korea then radically changed its policy. Park Chung-hee declared in June 1973 that South Korea would no longer oppose the admission of North Korea to the United Nations or other international organizations; he added that dual membership in the UN for the two Koreas should be regarded as an interim measure pending unification of the country. North Korea denounced the concept of dual UN membership as designed to perpetuate the division of Korea.

In 1975 the UN General Assembly passed rival resolutions on the Korean issue, even though the actions called for were in some respects contradictory. The resolution favoring North Korea called for the dissolution of the UN Command, the withdrawal of U.S. forces from Korea, and the replacement of the Korean armistice agreement by a peace treaty between North Korea and the United States. The resolution favoring South Korea also proposed the dissolution of the UN Command, but only if the parties concerned agreed that the provisions of the armistice agreement remained in force. (The resolution noted that the United States and the Republic of Korea intended to designate military officers as "successors in command" to assume the responsibility for supervision of the armistice previously exercised by the UN Command.)

Secretary of State Henry Kissinger, in his speech at the United Nations, proposed that the two Koreas, the United States, and the People's Republic of China meet to discuss alternative ways to maintain the armistice, possibly following this meeting with a wider conference including the Soviet Union and Japan. He also advocated membership for both Koreas in the UN and the establishment of diplomatic relations with both Koreas by the United States, the Soviet Union, China, and Japan. These proposals have been reiterated by the Carter administration, but North Korea and its allies have rejected them, and the stalemate over Korea continues.

In the contest for bilateral diplomatic relations, North Korea gained on South Korea up to December 1976, at which time 94 nations maintained relations with Seoul and 90 with Pyongyang. Subsequently, however, South Korea has gained ground, boosting its total to 102 as of January 1978, as compared with 92 for North Korea. Now 53 states maintain relations with both Koreas, and the trend toward dual recognition appears to be continuing.

Although North Korea was admitted to the group of nonaligned nations in 1975 and South Korea was excluded, Seoul's recent expansion of bilateral relations with members of the nonaligned group has alarmed Pyongyang. In February 1978 the North Korean government sent a long memorandum to countries with which it had diplomatic relations, warning them against maintaining relations with South Korea. The memorandum was followed up by a flurry of visits to Asian and African countries by high-level officials. North Korea's credentials as a "revolutionary" Third World state give it a political advantage over South Korea in some countries, but South Korea's economic strength and its rapidly expanding international network of trade and business contacts place it in a stronger position for the long run in the contest for international status.

Choices for Americans

The withdrawal of all U.S. forces from mainland Southeast Asia after the fall of Saigon in 1975 focused attention on Korea, the only remaining portion of the Asian mainland where the United States maintained military forces. Some Americans, doubting that U.S. interests in South Korea justified continuing to run the risk of having to fight another war there, advocated military disengagement from that country. Others argued that the defeat in Vietnam made it essential for the United States to hold firm in Korea. The debate over strategic interests was complicated by the distaste many Americans felt for the repressive actions taken by Park Chung-hee to strengthen his position and by Korean attempts to influence members of Congress with money. President Carter's middle-of-the-road policy of gradual withdrawal of U.S. ground forces was criticized by some for going too far and by others for not going far enough. There were no easy choices. Whichever policy the United States chose to follow toward Korea would carry with it costs and risks that were difficult to appraise.

Disengagement

Those favoring total withdrawal of American military forces from South Korea argue that the costs and risks of that course of action would be lower than those of remaining involved. Some base their advocacy of military disengagement on the assumption that the South Koreans, possessing a much larger population and economy than North Korea, can defend themselves, especially if the United States withdraws its forces gradually and helps the South Koreans build up their own forces. Others advocate withdrawal whether or not the South Koreans can defend themselves, on the ground that U.S. interests in Korea do not justify the continued risk of being drawn into war there. They point out that U.S. economic interests in South Korea are relatively small and that an attack on South Korea would not directly threaten the security of the United States. Furthermore, they deny that the admittedly much more important U.S. economic and security interests in Japan would be severely damaged if the withdrawal of U.S. forces from South Korea should result in the conquest of the Peninsula by North Korea. While conceding that Japanese economic interests in South Korea would suffer, advocates of this view believe that the Japanese would adjust to a unified communist Korea as they have adjusted to communist China and communist Vietnam, and that they would do so without losing confidence in the U.S. commitment to defend Japan.

Some supporters of U.S. disengagement advance the view that the Japanese should undertake the responsibility of helping in South Korea's defense in the place of Americans, since South Korea is clearly more important to Japan than to the United States. Those holding this view are not concerned that such a commitment would result in a more heavily armed Japan, perhaps equipped with nuclear weapons. They regard the consequences of that development as potentially less damaging to the United States than the risk of being involved in war in Korea.

Park Chung-hee's treatment of the opposition has strengthened the proponents of U.S. disengagement. Many oppose continuing a U.S. commitment to help defend an authoritarian government in Seoul either on moral grounds or because they view such a government as inherently unstable.

Policy of the Carter Administration

The Carter administration, like its predecessors, regards the defense of South Korea as a vital U.S. security interest and rejects the idea of disengagement. The security of South Korea and Japan are considered so closely intertwined that American failure to ensure the defense of South Korea would gravely weaken Japanese confidence in the U.S. commitment to the security of Japan. The risk would be great that the Japanese would then feel the need to rearm heavily, possibly with nuclear weapons, and the equilibrium that prevails among the big powers in East Asia today would be upset, with unpleasant and potentially disastrous consequences.

Although committed to ensuring the security of South Korea, President Carter has concluded, as did President Nixon when he withdrew the U.S. Seventh Division in 1971, that fewer U.S. troops will be needed to achieve that purpose. Consequently, he has announced the withdrawal of all U.S. ground combat forces from South Korea and has worked out a plan with the South Korean government to complete the withdrawal by 1982, with the last two brigades of the U.S. Second Division, the principal U.S. ground combat force in Korea, to remain until near the end of the withdrawal period. In the meantime, the South Korean army will be strengthened so as to compensate for the removal of the Second Division's firepower. Much of the Second Division's equipment, valued at $800 million, is to be turned over to the Koreans, and $275 million is to be made available in foreign military sales credits in the 1979 fiscal year, with comparable credits to be provided for several subsequent years. Twelve F-4s are to be added to the U.S. tactical fighter wing stationed in South Korea, which will remain after U.S. ground forces are withdrawn. The original plan contemplated the withdrawal of 6000 U.S. troops in 1978, but delay in congressional authorization of the equipment transfer caused the President to withdraw only about 3000 men in 1978.

President Carter based his decision to withdraw U.S. ground combat troops on the judgment that the South Korean army of 520,000 can withstand a North Korean attack with only U.S. air, naval, and logistic support if it receives additional equipment. The relocation of the Second Division in the United States has the added advantage of making it available for deployment anywhere in the world where a crisis might arise. Tactical nuclear weapons located in Korea for use by U.S. ground forces presumably will be withdrawn also. Their deterrent value is questionable, because of the improbability that an American President would be wil'ing to accept the international political costs of ordering the use of nuclear weapons for the first time in over 30 years, especially against a small Asian country armed only with conventional weapons.

In order to convince the North Koreans that the United States remains committed to the defense of South Korea despite the withdrawal of its ground units, joint maneuvers will be carried out frequently with South Korean forces. One such maneuver in March 1978, the largest joint exercise since the Korean war, demonstrated the ability of the United States to bring powerful air and sea forces rapidly from the continental United States, Hawaii, Guam, Japan, and the Philippines and concentrate them in and around Korea.

Although the Carter administration has strongly emphasized its opposition to violations of human rights throughout the world, it has not attempted to compel Park Chung-hee to modify his domestic policies by withholding or threatening to withhold military support for South Korea. U.S. officials believe that the United States can exert more influence on the conduct of the South Korean government by quiet persuasion behind the scenes than by provoking a confrontation that would increase the risk of political disorder and might invite intervention by North Korea.

The South Korean government has reluctantly acquiesced in the U.S. decision to withdraw its ground forces, provided additional military equipment is made available as promised. Privately, however, South Korean government officials continue to express fear that the removal of U.S. troops from their front-line position will increase the risk of a North Korean attack, and similar misgivings are voiced freely by opposition leaders and by the Seoul press. Frequently the view is expressed in the United States, South Korea, and Japan that President Carter decided on the force withdrawal primarily to carry out a campaign promise and that he made the decision hastily, without adequate preparation or consultation with the South Koreans and Japanese.

Maximum Deterrence

Some Americans have taken issue with President Carter's withdrawal policy on the ground that it unduly increases the risk of an attack by Kim Il-sung's forces. For 25 years, they maintain, the presence of American ground forces between Seoul and the DMZ has deterred Kim from attacking because American involvement in the combat was certain. The involvement of U.S. air and naval forces, located some distance from the front, cannot be counted on with the same certainty. Opponents of the Carter withdrawal program argue that the United States should avoid any step that would increase the risk of conflict even slightly, since the costs would be so great. They stress the fact that Seoul, with a fifth of South Korea's population, and much of its industry, is only 25 miles from the DMZ and offers Kim a great temptation for a surprise attack. They also call attention to the opposition to the withdrawal policy among Koreans and Japanese in asserting that the costs and risks of the withdrawal outweigh any advantages. If the withdrawal is to be carried out, they say, at the very least some price should be extracted from the North Koreans in exchange. The withdrawal policy is also criticized for compelling the South Koreans to expand their arms production, thus accelerating the arms race on the peninsula, and for increasing the risk that the South Koreans might produce nuclear weapons.

Most critics of the Carter administration's withdrawal policy primarily are concerned that it may increase the risk of war. Some, however, oppose the reduction of U.S. forces because they fear it will lead to intensified repression of opponents of the Park government and will reduce U.S. influence on that government. They note that Park's political opponents also oppose the withdrawal of U.S. ground forces. They prefer that ground forces be left in Korea and urge the U.S. government to employ economic and other pressures to compel Park to liberalize the political system in South Korea.

5 American Perceptions

As in the case of Japan, discussed in chapter 4, relations between the United States and Korea depend on both current realities and the views of the American people. How do Americans perceive the current state of ties between these countries? What do Americans think of the Koreans and of certain policies of the two Korean governments? How supportive are Americans of our military commitments to South Korea? Compared with other countries, where do South Korea and North Korea rank in importance to Americans?

Summary of Views on Korea

The views of Americans toward Korea, as they emerged from our survey taken in mid-1978, may be summarized as follows: not unexpectedly, in view of "Koreagate" and considerable media attention to reported violations of human rights in the Republic of Korea, Americans are restrained in their warmth toward, and support for, our ally on the Korean peninsula. Views toward North Korea are far more negative. Americans rank both countries relatively low in terms of their importance to U.S. global interests.

Americans are not well informed about a number of specific issues concerning Korea, especially the relative economic development of North and South Korea, and the extent of trade between the United States and South Korea.

In terms of military and economic support for South Korea, Americans are ambivalent. While a plurality believes that the amount of U.S. military and economic assistance given to South Korea in the 25 years since the Korean armistice has been about right, a similar plurality believes that further aid should be withheld as a lever to make the Korean government cooperate fully in getting to the bottom of the "Koreagate" investigation.

A majority of Americans feel that U.S. force commitments in Korea should be kept at the present level or increased and oppose President Carter's announced plans to withdraw all remaining ground troops from South Korea. About half of the population, however, is opposed to the United States coming to the defense of South Korea in the event of renewed attack from the north, even though a majority favors defending Japan against aggression by either the Soviet Union or the People's Republic of

China. This may reflect acceptance by the American people of a variation of deterrence—since the presence of U.S. forces on the peninsula has been instrumental in maintaining the peace to date, why jeopardize that peace by removing one source of stability? But if that prop is removed, Americans add, and hostilities recur, then sentiment against U.S. reengagement in Korea prevails.

That Americans want to have their cake and eat it, too, may not be an unnatural sentiment. But it also suggests that the Carter administration has a major job of public education on its hands, if it wants Americans to realize that foreign policy planning cannot follow such inconsistent lines. American economic and security interests in the Republic of Korea are high; and a free and independent South Korea, in concert with a free and independent Japan, is central to peace in that troubled area of the globe. South Korea once was declared to be outside the U.S. defense perimeter, with tragic consequences. Americans and Congress must recognize that this mistake should not be repeated.

Let us now turn from this summary to look at American attitudes on some specific issues in the bilateral Seoul-Washington link.

Knowledge of Korea

In order to establish a setting for these views, we posed a number of questions to test awareness of and knowledge about Korea.

Geography

The first question dealt with geography.

> *When you think of Korea as a whole, that is both North and South Korea, which one statement on this card is correct?*

Korea has a common land boundary with India.	4%
Korea is a peninsula with a common land boundary with Communist China.	60
Korea is an island.	12
Korea has a common land boundary with Japan.	15
Don't know.	9

Although only six Americans in ten respond correctly, another 27 percent either see Korea as an island (Korea is a peninsula, after all, and thus largely surrounded by water) or geographically associate it closely with

Japan. Men and Americans 30 to 49 years of age, both of whom may have more enduring memories of the Korean war than others, are more knowledgeable; among them, 68 percent answer correctly. The college-educated do even better: more than three in four (76 percent) are correct.

Ideology

Americans appear to be more aware of the nature of the government in North Korea than the one in South Korea.

As you probably know, for many years two rival governments have called themselves Korea: on one hand, the Democratic People's Republic of Korea (or North Korea) in the northern part of the Korean peninsula, and, on the other, the Republic of Korea (or South Korea) in the south. Do you happen to know if North Korea does or does not have a communist government?

Yes, communist	65%
No, not communist	5
Don't know	30

And does South Korea have a communist government or not?

Yes, communist	16%
No, not communist	52
Don't know	32

Only a bare majority (52 percent) are aware that the staunchly anticommunist government of President Park in the south is not communist, hardly a very impressive showing. The one well-informed group is the college-educated, 74 percent of whom know that the government is not communist. A striking aspect of the ignorance about the South Korean government is the very large numbers of respondents who said they "don't know." The proportion who have no opinion is at least 24 percent in every group except the college-educated (of whom 15 percent "don't know") and reaches 65 percent among those with a grade school education.

Substantially more Americans (65 percent) know that the government in the north is communist, including 83 percent of the college-educated. But overall the numbers of "don't knows" is also high—30 percent.

Economic Development

Lack of knowledge of Korea includes economic affairs. Only about one American in three realizes that South Korea has outstripped North Korea economically:

From what you have read or heard, which do you think is more advanced economically, North Korea or South Korea, or are they about even in terms of economic development?

North Korea	14%
South Korea	32
Both about even	23
Don't know	31

Even among the college-educated, less than a majority (42 percent) are accurately informed about the economic advances in the south. Once again, those who "don't know" represent a large—and in many demographic subgroups the largest—proportion.

Trade with the United States

Given this misinformation about the relative economic development of North and South Korea, it is not in the least surprising that Americans are unusually uninformed about the extent of U.S. trade with South Korea:

The United States has trading and commercial relations with almost every country in the world. In terms of our trade with South Korea, that is, the total amount of goods that we sell to South Korea and buy from South Korea, which of the statements listed on this card do you think is the most accurate?

South Korea is one of our top 15 trading partners.	14%
South Korea is one of our top 49 trading partners but is not in the top 15.	26
South Korea is one of our top 75 trading partners but is not in the top 40.	16
South Korea is not one of our top 75 trading partners.	11
Don't know.	33

Only about one American in seven (14 percent) realizes that South Korea is now one of our 15 largest trading partners. (It is, in fact, four-teenth.) That extremely low level of awareness holds true in roughly equal measure for all the groups in our sample. Once again, it is the "don't knows" who predominate (33 percent), further evidence of how remarkably uninformed Americans are about South Korea.

Sources of Information

Where do Americans get their information, in so far as they have it, about South Korea?

Of the following, which are your main sources of awareness about South Korea? Please pick the one or two most important to you.

Television and radio	65%
Newspapers, magazines, and books	50
Movies	—
Purchase and use of South Korean goods	5
Personal contacts with South Koreans	3
Don't know	7

Television and radio predominate strongly among all groups but one—the college-educated get as much of their information about South Korea from newspapers, magazines, and books (64 percent in both cases). Although our survey did not go into this, one is tempted to speculate that "Koreagate" and "M*A*S*H" most importantly shape the views of most Americans about Korea. If this is so, the result would be a largely negative image—more so in the case of "Koreagate" perhaps, but also true for a television series set during the Korean war, with all the negative reminders that carries.

"Koreagate"

Responses to the following question make clear that public awareness of "Koreagate" is high.

Have you heard or read about charges that some South Koreans have tried to influence U.S. policy toward South Korea by making payments and giving favors to members of Congress and others in Washington?

Yes	73%
No	18
Don't know	9

The only groups where significantly more than 18 percent have not heard about the charges of influence buying are those with a grade school education and Americans 18 to 29 years of age—31 and 27 percent, respectively. Among the college-educated, more than nine in ten (91 percent) have heard of this major stumbling block in our bilateral relations. While much of the reporting on the scandal has reflected poorly on Congress, to be sure, there can be little doubt that it has also badly damaged the public's image of South Korea.

General Impressions of Korea

"Koreagate" aside, these responses suggest that Americans are not well informed about a number of basic issues concerning Korea. How, then, do Americans feel about North and South Korea and relations with our ally in the south?

Popularity

One question probed general attitudes toward both countries. Comparable figures are included for Japan, obtained during our April 1978 survey, and for the People's Republic of Korea on the mainland and the Republic of China on Taiwan, obtained in an earlier Potomac Associates survey conducted in April 1977.

	South Korea	North Korea	Japan	Republic of China	People's Republic of China
Very favorable	7%	1%	22%	15%	4%
Somewhat favorable	45	12	50	41	22
Somewhat unfavorable	20	35	13	13	29
Very unfavorable	7	30	4	5	23
Don't know	21	22	11	26	22

South Korea ranks well behind both Japan and the Republic of China on Taiwan, but ahead of the People's Republic of China, with North Korea firmly lodged in last place.

The more favorable attitude toward South than North Korea is especially strong among Americans with a college education: 61 percent of them view South Korea either very or somewhat favorably (9 points above the national average), while 79 percent see North Korea either somewhat or very unfavorably (14 points above the nation as a whole).

U.S.-Korean Relations

Our survey shows, however, that Americans are tempered in their reading of the current state of relations between the United States and South Korea—an assessment that most objective observers would share.

Do you feel that, at the present time, relations between the United States and South Korea are excellent, good, only fair, or poor?

Excellent	2%
Good	27
Only fair	42
Poor	11
Don't know	18

Nor are Americans particularly sanguine about what the future holds for ties between the two countries.

Over the next few years, do you expect relations between the United States and South Korea to get better, get worse, or stay about the same as they are now?

Get better	15%
Get worse	17
Stay about the same	47
Don't know	21

Overall, the appraisal of current relations is a somber one: 53 percent characterize present ties as either only fair or poor, whereas just 29 percent see them as good or excellent. Looking to the future, the situation is a virtual standoff: approximately one American in two (47 percent) anticipates no change, while the remainder who have opinions are split about equally between those who foresee improvement (15 percent) and those who expect a deterioration (17 percent).

An optimist might argue that these results are, in fact, somewhat better than expected, given the extensive and negative publicity surrounding "Koreagate." This would appear to be particularly true concerning attitudes about the future. If one chooses to call the glass half full rather than half empty, then one can say that a clear majority (62 percent) looks for relations to either stay the same or improve over the next few years. This majority may well believe that the influence-buying scandal will recede into the background and the two nations will then get on with other, more constructive business.

Human Rights

Considerable media coverage has been given to reported violations of human rights in both North and South Korea in recent years. On this score, the impressions are less favorable to the north than to the south.

Now I am going to ask you specifically your impression of the situation in South Korea and North Korea today as it concerns the human rights issue, that is, the degree to which the rights and liberties of their

*individual citizens are protected. First, what is your impression about
the situation in South Korea concerning human rights—very favorable,
somewhat favorable, somewhat unfavorable, or very unfavorable?*

*And what is your impression of the situation in North Korea
concerning human rights—very favorable, somewhat favorable,
somewhat unfavorable, or very unfavorable?*

	South Korea	*North Korea*
Very favorable	4%	1%
Somewhat favorable	27	8
Somewhat unfavorable	22	22
Very unfavorable	12	32
Don't know	35	37

In the case of South Korea, there is almost a standoff between those
who hold favorable views (31 percent) and those whose views are unfavorable (33 percent). On the other hand, at the two extremes opinion is
weighted to one side: those who say "very unfavorable" outnumber those
who say "very favorable" by a margin of 3 to 1 (12 percent to 4 percent). As
frequently has been the case, the largest single group—35 percent—has no
opinion on the issue of human rights in South Korea.

Attitudes concerning human rights in North Korea are significantly
more negative, although the "don't knows" also represent the largest single
bloc (37 percent). But the gap between those who hold positive and negative
views is great—54 percent say the situation in the north is unfavorable,
while only 9 percent term it favorable. Among the college-educated the division is even wider: 67 percent are negative, and only 8 percent positive. To
the extent that the Carter administration's emphasis on human rights has
struck a responsive chord with the American people, these findings suggest
a plus for South Korea when the situation there is contrasted with that of
North Korea. But when Americans consider the human rights issue in terms
of South Korea alone, they find the picture marginally negative.

Bilateral Issues

Even since the end of the Korean war, relations between the United States
and South Korea have been dominated by considerations of military security and economic assistance. These matters were explored in some depth in
our survey.

Amount of Aid

As far as military and economic assistance to South Korea is concerned, a
plurality of Americans feel that the United States has done about what it
should have:

In the 25 years since the Korean armistice, the United States has provided substantial military and economic assistance to South Korea, to help South Korea develop and to protect our own security interests in Asia. Do you think the amount of assistance we have provided to achieve these purposes has been pretty much on target, or has it not been the right amount?

Right amount	47%
Not right amount	23
Don't know	30

That almost half the population (47 percent) thinks our aid efforts have been about right is a mild surprise, in view of the general antipathy that so many Americans have for foreign aid programs. It is likely that responses to this question were given without full knowledge of the volume of this aid: the large number of respondents who say they "don't know" indicates the degree of ignorance on this subject.

Among those who think the United States has not provided the right amount of aid, the vast majority think we went too far, as responses to the following question (posed only to those who said "not the right amount") make clear:

Do you think we have given the South Koreans more than they have needed, so that they have taken advantage of us, or do you think that the South Koreans have developed quite well and have been loyal allies, and we have not given them enough?

Given too much	82%
Not given enough	12
Don't know	6

Aid and "Koreagate"

A remarkably large proportion of Americans (73 percent), as we noted earlier, at least are aware of the charges against some South Koreans of influence buying in Washington. Are Americans ready to penalize South Korea for its actions in regard to the investigation of these charges?

As you may know, charges have been made that some South Koreans have tried to influence the U.S. policy toward South Korea by making payments and giving other favors to members of Congress and others in Washington. Do you feel we should hold up the military and the economic aid we are now providing South Korea until we are satisfied its government is helping us fully to get to the bottom of these charges, or do you feel safeguarding South Korea from possible attack is too important to our own national security interests to hold up on military and economic aid for this reason?

Should hold up on aid   45%
Should continue to give aid   33
Don't know   22

Although a plurality (45 percent) favor using aid as a lever against Seoul in seeking a resolution of the "Koreagate" affair, the margin is not overwhelmingly one-sided. Interestingly, one group is opposed, though narrowly, to invoking the aid weapon—those with a college education, who are among the best informed about international affairs and who presumably are most swayed by considerations of U.S. security interests.

Troop Withdrawal

We noted earlier that most Americans favor maintaining or increasing U.S. troop levels in South Korea, but that at the same time a majority oppose defending South Korea against attack from the north. These questions were asked, however, in an unspecified context, without bringing into play Carter administration policies. In order to test sentiment within the framework of expressed presidential plans, we posed the following query:

As you may know, President Carter announced his intention to withdraw the remaining ground forces from South Korea over the next five years or so, while keeping U.S. naval and air forces there. Do you think we should go ahead and withdraw our ground troops, or do you think we need to keep some of our ground troops there?

Should withdraw   35%
Should keep some troops there   52
Don't know   13

In reply to the earlier question, 55 percent of the sample want American forces in South Korea either kept at the present level or increased, while 34 percent called for a reduction or termination of that commitment. Introducing the fact of presidential intent and policy appears to have little effect on how Americans approach the troop withdrawal issue. The college-educated are somewhat more in favor of the Carter withdrawal policy than the nation as a whole, but even so they remain opposed by a distinct majority of 53 to 42 percent. Furthermore, the President's party does not seem swayed by his endorsement of troop withdrawal: Democrats are opposed by a 53 to 34 percent majority, as are Republicans by 58 to 33 percent.

Reengagement of U.S. Troops

If it is assumed that troop withdrawal is carried out, opposition to reengagement in Korea should North Korea attack remains essentially unchanged from the levels reported earlier.

> *Assuming that the United States does withdraw all its ground forces from South Korea, our naval and air forces still would be involved in the defense of South Korea. If North Korea should attack, and South Korea was being defeated by North Korea, would you favor or would you oppose sending U.S. ground troops back to support South Korea?*

Would favor sending troops	31%
Would oppose sending troops	49
Don't know	20

Responses to this question are virtually uniform among all groups. Party affiliation again has almost no effect, a factor that could be important if Congress were faced with an actual decision. Thus Republicans are opposed by a margin of 48 to 33 percent; Democrats, 49 to 30 percent; and Independents, 50 to 30 percent.

Support for the continued presence of U.S. ground forces in South Korea, coupled with unwillingness to get involved should hostilities occur after a planned troop withdrawal is completed, suggested anew that Americans may well have fashioned their own variant of deterrence. Since the peace-keeping role of the American military establishment in South Korea has proven effective thus far, why risk the possible consequences of troop withdrawal? Should President Carter decide to stretch out the withdrawal program or leave a significant contingent of American ground troops in South Korea indefinitely, it does not appear that he will run into a groundswell of public opposition.

6 A Look to the Future

Since the end of the Korean war and the institution of an armistice arrangement intended to be temporary, yet lasting more than 25 years, United States' policy toward the Korean peninsula has focused heavily on bilateral relations between Washington and Seoul. Particular attention has been paid to strategic and military considerations and the buildup of the South Korean armed forces and economy. The search for a political settlement that would reduce hostility between the two Koreas and lessen the danger of renewed conflict has been overshadowed by the immediate requirement of maintaining a balance of military force to deter aggression.

It is time, we believe, for American policy to take greater account of long-term considerations. This means, first and foremost, the development of a clearer picture of what would be the most desirable arrangement on the peninsula as a whole. U.S. actions, such as the proposed withdrawal of ground forces, could then be made an integral part of a comprehensive program to achieve such an outcome.

Given the implacable hostility between the governments in Seoul and Pyongyang and the conviction of each that it alone is the true claimant to authority over all Korea, unification of the peninsula appears for the foreseeable future to lie beyond the realm of what is possible, not to mention likely. Neither President Park nor President Kim (nor presumably any logical successor) can entertain the notion of a country unified under the leadership of the other side. Under these circumstances, unification could be achieved only through resort to arms. The policy of the United States toward the Korean peninsula aims at preventing the outbreak of renewed hostilities. Both the Soviet Union and the People's Republic of China appear to have adopted similar policies of restraint.

If unification, however desirable, is excluded as a feasible alternative, then it is in the best interests of all concerned to move toward a more durable stabilization of relations between the two countries. The goal should be to minimize the risk of war, turn the border area into a zone of relative tranquility and interchange, foster the growth of direct communications and exchange between north and south, and ultimately lead to an acceptance by South Korea and North Korea of the right of the other to exist in a competitive relationship. Cross recognition by the big powers and membership of both Koreas in the United Nations, however hard to envisage now, could become realities. Since 1973 South Korea and its supporters have advocated these policies; it remains to convince North Korea and its backers.

In supporting a possible long-term trend along these lines, it is incumbent on the United States to make clear its unwavering commitment to the integrity of South Korea and willingness to back South Korea in the protection of its independence. South Korea's exposed geographic position and unique location at a point on the globe where the political, economic, and security interests of the United States, Japan, the Soviet Union, and the People's Republic of China intersect, make it mandatory, in our view, that U.S. policy be prudent, realistic, and firm, so as not to invite missteps by South Korea, North Korea, or any outside parties.

A comprehensive, long-term U.S. policy toward Korea that would be supported by a majority of the American people could be based on the following guidelines.

(1) The Asian-Pacific region is growing faster economically than any other region of the world and probably will continue to do so. Already U.S. trade with this region surpasses its trade with Western Europe. South Korea, a dynamic nation of 35 million, has had one of the fastest growing economies in the world in recent years. It is becoming increasingly tightly linked with Japan and other East Asian countries. The new, outward-looking policy of the People's Republic of China is likely to create an increasingly complex, mutually beneficial network of economic and other relationships between Japan and China and between the United States and China. Peace in northeast Asia is essential if the United States is to benefit from these trends. Continued U.S. security commitments and force deployments in this region probably will be necessary for a long time in order to maintain the existing equilibrium among the four big powers. Total military disengagement from South Korea would increase the risk of war and have such a destabilizing impact on Japan and other countries of the region that it is not a practicable policy.

(2) The planned, gradual withdrawal of the U.S. ground combat forces from South Korea is unlikely to be disruptive, provided certain conditions are met. First, Congress must furnish the compensatory arms package for South Korean forces now contemplated. In addition, the balance of forces on the peninsula and other circumstances should be reappraised before the last units are withdrawn in 1982, to determine that the risk of renewed conflict remains low. Among the factors to be considered in such an appraisal is the progress—or lack of it—toward agreements between the two Koreas and among the big powers for a lasting peace on the Korean peninsula, as discussed below. The views held by Americans concerning the level of U.S. forces in Korea appear to allow the President considerable flexibilty in adjusting the timing of the withdrawal to suit prevailing conditions.

(3) High-level consultations should be held among the United States,

South Korea, and Japan, following appropriate working-level preparations, to develop a program of diplomatic actions for the period of U.S. ground force withdrawal. The objectives of the program would be to convince the People's Republic of China, the Soviet Union, and North Korea that it would be in their interests to join with the United States, Japan, and South Korea in measures to reduce the risk of war and facilitate peaceful coexistence of the two Koreas. A variety of approaches might be considered: tripartite talks among the United States and the two Koreas, quadripartite talks with the addition of the People's Republic of China, and larger conferences including Japan and the Soviet Union. The United States, Japan, and South Korea should coordinate and intensify their efforts to broaden international support for a revitalized and constructive dialogue between the two Koreas, international agreement on updated truce arrangements, admission of the two Koreas to the United Nations, and cross recognition by the big powers.

(4) An accelerated arms race on the peninsula is a real danger and to some degree a present reality. Since South Korea is determined to catch up with North Korea in arms production, it is not likely that an arms race could be checked by the United States' reversing its decision to withdraw its ground forces. But we should try to impress moderation on South Korea and seek an agreement with the Soviet Union and China not to supply advanced weapons to either country.

(5) Our policy should continue to impede steps by South Korea to produce nuclear weapons. The United States has strong leverage with which to prevent such a development, including both its defense support and its role as a supplier of enriched uranium for South Korea's power industry.

(6) The United States should continue to make known to the South Korean government that violations of human rights endanger close relations between our two countries. Growing intercourse between South Korea and the industrial democracies will increase pressure among Koreans themselves for greater liberalization of their political system, just as Korea's dramatic economic development has brought substantial improvement in the quality of life of most Korean citizens. In voicing concern for human rights, the United States should proceed with appropriate discretion and recognition of those gains that are made; too direct intervention and pressure from the United States are likely to provoke nationalistic reactions and prove counterproductive.

(7) The growing economic gap between South Korea and North Korea (with the tide running in South Korea's favor), the potential in a few years' time for equalization of their military production capabilities, and the progress by Seoul in expanding its diplomatic relations with other countries will contribute markedly to South Korea's self-esteem and self-confidence. In terms of its relations with North Korea, this could prove to be a double-

edged sword. On one hand, it might permit enhanced diplomatic flexibility on Seoul's part, thereby improving prospects for intercourse between north and south. On the other hand—and this second possibility should not be underestimated—a robust and dominant South Korea could decide to harden its negotiating stance and consider resorting to threatening demands and pressures. The United States' policy should be to encourage the former and discourage the latter.

(8) In view of the continuing mutual interests that will link the United States and South Korea, extensive and sophisticated efforts are needed from both sides to improve the climate of understanding and awareness between our two countries. The serious gaps in Americans' knowledge of Korea that our survey has demonstrated need to be addressed, perhaps through new or additional cultural, intellectual, and other exchange programs. It is clear that Americans do not fully comprehend the extent of our economic relations with Korea, and the distinction they draw between the security of South Korea as compared to Japan is not in keeping with the realities of maintaining peace in that area. The field is open to a variety of innovative educational and information efforts. At the same time, each side must approach its activities in the other's country with a degree of maturity and mutual respect that has not always characterized such undertakings in the past.

Part III:
China

7 Policy Setting

President Carter and his advisers confront a dilemma in trying to move ahead on China policy. The problem is how to "normalize" relations with the world's most populous country, the People's Republic of China (PRC), while still trying to maintain economic, cultural, and perhaps even military ties to the smaller Republic of China (ROC) on Taiwan.

This dilemma has not been resolved in the first years of the Carter administration. Indeed, China policy has been overshadowed by other issues—frustrating negotiations over SALT II with the Soviets, a hard-fought victory on a new Panama Canal treaty, diplomatic and military balancing acts in the Middle East, a quandary over dealing with Soviet and Cuban pressures in the horn of Africa and the sub-Sahara, and economic and military tensions in the alliances with Western Europe and Japan. And often such questions have been intertwined with the administration's commitment to human rights diplomacy.

In this array of foreign initiatives, where does China fit? Although China has been a policy question of secondary importance to the Carter administration, it has not been ignored altogether. Several times in his campaign and his Presidency, Carter reaffirmed the U.S. commitment to the Shanghai Communiqué and to the eventual "normalization of relations" with Peking. On the other hand, he has refused to specify a timetable and has expressed concern for the "security of the people of Taiwan." In early 1977 Carter's son Chip visited China, and former United Auto Workers President Leonard Woodcock was appointed head of the U.S. Liaison Office in Peking (the current substitute for a formal embassy). In August 1977 Secretary of State Vance went to China on a trip that prompted mixed reactions: Carter claimed that it had achieved "substantial progress" while Chinese Vice Chairman Teng Hsiao-p'ing called it a "setback" in Sino-American relations. After a fall and winter of fence mending, the pace of diplomacy picked up again in early 1978 in the context of deteriorating U.S.-Soviet relations. In an April press conference, the President suggested that normalization of relations with the PRC might come in a "matter of months." In May the Chinese appointed a prominent diplomat, Chai Tse-min, to be head of the PRC Liaison Office in Washington, a post that had been vacant for six months. Also in May 1978 National Security Adviser Zbigniew Brzezinski made a trip to Peking which apparently yielded broad agreement on strategic issues, though no overt progress on normalization.

But the tough questions surrounding China policy are still to be addressed. Will the administration actively seek normal diplomatic relations with the PRC, or will it attempt to perpetuate the status quo détente without normalization? If it seeks normalization with the mainland, how will it protect American security and commercial interests with Taiwan? What does the President see as the possible benefits and liabilities, both short-term and long-term, of normalized Sino-American relations? How will China policy fit into the broader Asian and global policy objectives of the Carter administration—including détente with the Soviet Union, close ties with a nonmilitarized Japan, stability in East Asia (particularly in Korea), improved north-south relations, and constructive multilateral negotiations on arms control, energy resources, and food supply?

President Carter and his advisers must also ponder the policies of his predecessors and the recent history of Sino-American détente. What has happened since Ping-Pong diplomacy in 1971? What are the Nixon and Ford legacies in Sino-American relations? Can President Carter put a distinctive imprint on China policy, one that will win support from Congress and the public? A brief review of Sino-American relations since 1971 may help shed light on the policy alternatives facing Washington.

The Nixon Legacy

From the 1971-1974 Nixon years, Carter inherits the legacy of rapprochement between the United States and China. The emergence of détente with China was a dramatic and popular venture that contrasted sharply with the bleakest days of the Indochina war. An air of great expectations surrounded Ping-Pong diplomacy, Henry Kissinger's secret trip to Peking, the admission of the People's Republic to the United Nations, the widely publicized visit of President Nixon to China, and the issuance of the Shanghai Communiqué.

Nixon's statement at the end of his China trip that "this was a week that changed the world" may have overstated the case, but certainly the policy of détente opened a new chapter in Asian-American relations. From 1950 to 1971, the People's Republic and the United States had been at loggerheads around China's rim—open warfare in Korea from 1950 to 1953, the brink of war in the offshore islands crisis of 1958, and the constant danger of Chinese intervention in the Indochina war in the 1960s. Behind this military confrontation was an ideological conflict expressed by leaders on both sides with the intensity of a religious crusade. The American commitment to "containing Red China" and "supporting the Free World" was matched by the Chinese Communist commitment to "supporting wars of national liberation" and "opposing American imperialism and its running dogs."

Under détente, both countries veered from their collision course, toned down their ideological rhetoric, and began to explore cooperation rather than conflict. During the Nixon-Kissinger and Mao-Chou years, Sino-American détente rested on several parallel interests in the strategic realm: (1) opposition to Soviet expansionism, especially in Asia and the Pacific; (2) desire for American military withdrawal from Vietnam and from other parts of the Asian continent; (3) maintenance of a strong American naval and air presence in the Pacific to counteract possible Soviet expansion; (4) stability on the Korean peninsula to avoid the possibility of a war involving the United States, the People's Republic, and the USSR; (5) dealing with the Taiwan issue in a way that would not provoke Taiwan to pursue independence, develop a strong nuclear arms capability, or seek alliance with the USSR.

Discovery and pursuit of these parallel goals helped bring greater stability to Asian affairs in the early 1970s. But some of these goals were short-term in nature, and considerable progress has been made in several of these areas. Many also hinge on common Chinese and American tensions with the Soviet Union and thus are subject to the uncertainties of triangular politics. While concern about Soviet expansionism remains a key element in the foreign policy calculations of both Washington and Peking, it is unlikely to provide an enduring foundation for cordial, cooperative Sino-American relations. In short, while the Nixon-Kissinger and Mao-Chou teams opened the door to détente, they failed to leave their successors a clearly defined, longer-term agenda for bilateral and multilateral relations in Asian and global affairs.

Bilateral Sino-American relations in diplomacy, trade, and cultural and scientific exchanges have shown a pattern similar to their strategic relations—a peak of activity from 1972 to 1974, followed by a plateau and great uncertainty from 1975 to 1978. In the early 1970s, Sino-American détente was a powerful, new ingredient in world affairs, its chief architects still ruled in both Washington and Peking, and both sides assumed that diplomatic recognition would be forthcoming soon. Then in the mid-1970s, both countries became absorbed with the politics of domestic succession, and Sino-American rapprochement lost some of its momentum.

The Shanghai Communiqué issued jointly on February 28, 1972 set the diplomatic context and tone for the new era of détente and expressed the high expectations of leaders on both sides of the Pacific. The communiqué recognized that "there are essential differences between China and the United States in their social systems and foreign policies," but also committed both sides to international relations on the basis of "equality and mutual benefit, and peaceful coexistence." The communiqué stated that "the normalization of relations between the two countries is not only in the interest of the Chinese and American peoples but also contributes to the relaxation of tension in Asia and the world.'' On the difficult issue of Taiwan, the island home of the Republic of China (ROC) governed by the Chinese Nationalists and supported by diplomatic recognition and military treaty with the United States, both sides stated separate positions.

The Chinese side reaffirmed its position: The Taiwan question is the crucial question obstructing the normalization of relations between China and the United States; the government of the People's Republic of China is the sole legal government of China; Taiwan is a province which has long been returned to the motherland; the liberation of Taiwan is China's internal affair in which no other country has the right to interfere; and all U.S. forces and military installations must be withdrawn from Taiwan. The Chinese government firmly opposes any activities which aim at the creation of ''one China, one Taiwan,'' ''one China, two governments,'' ''two Chinas,'' an ''independent Taiwan'' or advocate that ''the status of Taiwan remains to be determined.''

The U.S. side declared: The United States acknowledges that all Chinese on either side of the Taiwan Strait maintain there is but one China and that Taiwan is part of China. The United States government does not challenge that position. It reaffirms its interest in a peaceful settlement of the Taiwan question by the Chinese themselves. With this prospect in mind, it affirms the ultimate objective of the withdrawal of all U.S. forces and military installations from Taiwan. In the meantime, it will progressively reduce its forces and military installations on Taiwan as the tension in the area diminishes.

In a concluding section of the communiqué, both countries agreed to explore exchanges in ''such fields as science, technology, culture, sports and journalism'' and to ''facilitate the progressive development of trade between their two countries.'' They also agreed to maintain diplomatic contacts ''for concrete consultations to further the normalization of relations.''

Washington and Peking moved quickly from 1972 to 1974 to fulfill the content and spirit of the Shanghai Communiqué. In 1973 liaison offices were established in Peking and Washington, both headed by senior diplomats; they have performed most of the functions of full-scale embassies. Some observers saw Peking's approval of liaison offices as a major Chinese concession, made in the expectation that normalized relations soon would follow. Secretary Kissinger, often accompanied by senior administration officials, began to include Peking as a frequent stop in his worldwide shuttle diplomacy. Several delegations of congressmen and senators in both political parties traveled to China; some of them prepared influential reports concerning their trips and U.S.-China relations.

Sino-American trade swelled from a mere $5 million in 1971 to $930 million by 1974 (roughly 90 percent of that trade was American exports to China, and almost half of the trade consisted of American agricultural products). Among other American exports were high-technology merchandise, such as Boeing 707 aircraft, Pratt and Whitney jet engines, and RCA satellite systems. Exchanges kept pace with trade and diplomacy. By 1975 several hundred Chinese had visited the United States, and roughly 10,000 Americans had journeyed to the PRC. Some exchanges had a spectacular quality—the Philadelphia Orchestra drew large audiences throughout Chinese cities, the televised performance of Chinese acrobats and a *wu-shu* troupe attracted considerable American attention, and the Chinese archaeological exhibit in 1975 brought record crowds to museums in the United States. In terms of popular interest, America seemed to be on a China high in the early 1970s.

The Ford Years

Since 1975, however, the Sino-American relationship has been on a plateau, and uncertainties and anxieties have become common. Although the number of travelers continued to increase (in all, roughly 1000 Chinese and 15,000 Americans from 1971 to early 1977), problems began to arise in cultural exchanges. In 1975 for instance, a visit of performing artists from the PRC was canceled because of the last-minute inclusion of a song about "liberating Taiwan." Also, a visit of American mayors to China was canceled because the Chinese objected to the inclusion of the mayor of San Juan, a gesture in keeping with their perception of Puerto Rican aspirations for independence. Sino-American trade fell precipitously to $336 million in 1976; most of this drop was due to improved harvests on the mainland and a resulting decline in the Chinese need for American agricultural products, as well as the Chinese desire for a balance in trade with the United States. Such a balance was achieved in 1976.

Behind these surface tensions in the mid-1970s were deeper problems centering on Taiwan and on leadership in both Peking and Washington. The Taiwan issue remains the Gordian knot in relations between the United States and the People's Republic. The Shanghai Communiqué demonstrated the gap between American and Chinese views but seemed to imply there was room for negotiation in the interest of normalizing relations. The United States reduced its troop strength on Taiwan from roughly 10,000 in 1972 to about 1400. U.S. diplomatic recognition and security treaty ties with the ROC, however, remained intact; moreover, American trade with Taiwan increased considerably since the early 1970s, reaching $4.8 billion in 1976, and several new ROC consulates opened in the United States. During 1975-1976, the PRC leadership demonstrated irritation in several ways over the slowness of U.S. moves toward resolution of the Taiwan question—a relatively cool and unproductive reception for

President Ford when he visited China in late 1975, a warm reception by Mao for former President Nixon in early 1976, and words of displeasure expressed in the Chinese media and to visiting Americans.

Leadership problems in both countries exacerbated difficulties over Taiwan.

According to reports in the American press, in the early 1970s President Nixon may have indicated privately to the Chinese his intention to achieve normal diplomatic relations during his administration. But Nixon soon became absorbed by the Watergate scandal, and his resignation in 1974 removed from power á President personally committed to better relations with the mainland. Gerald Ford, concerned about political attacks from the Republican right wing, was content to endorse the inherited Nixon policy of détente without making new initiatives towards Peking. The sudden American exit from Vietnam in early 1975 prompted Ford to be wary of a new approach on Taiwan since it might have been perceived as a further weakening in American commitments to Asian allies.

In China, 1976 was a year of political upheaval capped by the deaths of Mao and Chou, the fall of Vice Premier Teng Hsiao-p'ing, the emergence of Hua Kuo-feng as premier and then as party chairman, and the purge of Mao's widow as part of the radical faction called the "Gang of Four." Thus, as the Chinese leadership expressed annoyance about lack of U.S. moves toward normalization, they themselves also found it difficult to give sustained attention to policy toward the United States because of their turbulent internal politics.

Early Carter Years

Thus we come to the current state of Sino-American relations: détente still prevails, and a return to confrontation seems unlikely in the immediate future. But if the Nixon years were upbeat and the Ford years downbeat, it is difficult to describe the rhythm of Sino-American relations in the early Carter administration.

On a diplomatic level, the coolness of the late 1977 Vance trip was countered by the relative warmth of the early 1978 Brzezinski voyage. But it is difficult to determine whether such changes in atmosphere portend a shift toward full diplomatic relations. Hints of such a possibility emerged in June 1978 when American media sources reported that the Carter administration was considering its "three principles" for normalization: (1) the United States must be allowed to continue trade with and grant aid to Taiwan after full relations are restored with Peking—including military assistance; (2) a U.S. trade mission would be established in place of the existing embassy in Taipei; and (3) Peking must agree that force will not be used to reunite Taiwan with the mainland.

But such reports have not been verified, and we still remain in a stalemate, albeit a cordial one, seeking normalization of relations between Washington and Peking.

Economically the $375 million in two-way trade for 1977 continued the modest trade levels of the previous two years. But while the volume remained low, certain features of Sino-American commerce seemed more promising. As a result of mediocre harvests, Chinese orders for American farm produce, particularly cotton and bean oils, increased markedly in 1978 over previous years. China's renewed emphasis on industrial modernization forces it to look to the United States as a source of advanced technology, especially in the following areas: oil drilling equipment (manifested by the visit of a prestigious petroleum delegation to the United States and the purchase of offshore drilling rigs manufactured in Singapore by subsidiaries of American companies), steel production, microwave communications, and advanced computers (with possible defensive military application).

The pace of Sino-American exchanges picked up in 1978 as well. The PRC sent a very large performing arts troupe to demonstrate dance and music, some traditional as well as contemporary, in five American cities—the biggest Chinese spectacle since the archaeological exhibit of 1975. And the floodgates began to open to American tourism in China: an estimated 10,000 will visit China in 1978 (and some projections for 1979-1980 estimate 20,000 a year).

So even in this era of uncertainty about diplomatic relations, Americans and Chinese are getting to know each other a little better and finding that commerce offers some mutual benefits on a limited scale. Strategically, in great contrast to the 1950s and 1960s, Washington and Peking continue to find that their agreements outnumber their disagreements. Thus Peking applauds the continued U.S. military presence in Japan and the Philippines and firm American expressions of concern about Soviet expansion into Africa, South Asia, and Southeast Asia. The United States and China seem to have settled into a rather comfortable relationship, prompted by mutual strategic concerns and linked by limited commercial and cultural ties, altogether a remarkable transformation in a decade. But it is also a new, fragile relationship with the big questions of normalization and Taiwan yet to be resolved.

Policy Issues

What, then, are the major China policy considerations facing the Carter administration? Since Taiwan is clearly the most difficult issue, it will be considered fully in a separate section. But the questions of Taiwan and diplomatic recognition of Peking also must be considered in conjunction with broader American policy concerns in China, East Asia, the Pacific, and other parts of the globe.

Considered as an isolated question, U.S. diplomatic recognition of the People's Republic seems an eminently sensible policy and would appear long overdue. After all, the People's Republic is an established regime and has governed the population of the Chinese mainland, now numbering over 900 million, for over a quarter-century. Recognition does not imply U.S. approval of a particular country; rather it establishes regular diplomatic channels of communication and facilitates trade and other exchanges. The United States presently has diplomatic relations with most communist countries and has had such relations with the Soviet Union since 1933. And the United States is the only major world power which still lacks full diplomatic relations with the People's Republic.

It is Taiwan, the home of 17 million people, that complicates the situation. Peking demands that Washington sever its diplomatic relations and its military security treaty with Taipei if it wants to normalize relations with Peking. While the United States could probably retain its commercial and cultural ties with Taiwan, recognition of Peking necessitates derecognition of Taipei and the termination of a formal security treaty. Thus, the United States faces a complex and somewhat uncertain compromise over Taiwan in pursuing normalization with the mainland. Should the United States make that compromise? What are the key considerations beyond the Taiwan issue per se?

Détente without Normalization?

First, can Sino-American détente be perpetuated without normal diplomatic relations?[a]

Some opponents of normalization argue that the current status quo offers the best of all alternatives: multilevel relationships with Peking without selling out Taipei in the process. They argue that strategic and economic factors—Peking's concern about the Soviet threat and need for American technology—have overridden the issues of diplomatic recognition and Taiwan in clearing the way for detente. Furthermore, there is no certainty that Peking will be a more compatible partner in détente after normalization; indeed, the military and economic security of Taiwan might be threatened by the mainland Chinese after the United States loosens its ties with the island. A 1977 editorial in *The New York Times* summarized this

---

[a]In this section, it is impossible to include the whole spectrum of arguments from opponents and proponents of normalization. Instead we have discussed the most important arguments.

argument well when it invoked former Budget Director Burt Lance's homi-
ly, "If it ain't broke, don't fix it."

Proponents of normalization, on the other hand, contend that hopes
for resolution of the Taiwan question and for diplomatic relations were
major factors, along with strategic and economic considerations, behind
Peking's interest in détente. Sino-American rapprochement must be seen
against the legacy of a quarter-century of hostility and warfare. Without
normalization, so the argument goes, Washington's new relationship with
Peking is likely to deteriorate. China might well seek a separate rapprochement with the Soviet Union, looking to the Soviets and other Western nations for technology. In the worst case, a new generation of Chinese leaders
might rekindle the fires of anti-American nationalism in China, and the two
countries might become enemies once again. Americans might then look
back to the failure to normalize relations in the 1970s as a tragic "lost
chance."

Bilateral Benefits

A second question concerns the possible bilateral benefits of Sino-American
diplomatic relations.

Opponents of normalization hold that the United States already enjoys
a considerable array of bilateral contacts with the People's Republic and actually has closer ties with the mainland than many Western European countries with full diplomatic relations. The liaison offices in Peking and
Washington are embassies in all but name. American trade with the
People's Republic has prospered without diplomatic recognition; indeed, in
1974 America ranked third among China's trading partners after Japan and
Hong Kong. American cultural and educational exchanges with the PRC
have been surpassed in number only by the Japanese. Furthermore, there is
no guarantee that American trade and exchanges with the mainland would
increase after normalization; the experience of many countries has been just
the opposite. Most importantly, diplomatic recognition in quest of these
uncertain gains might jeopardize commercial relations with Taiwan, a much
more important trading partner.

Supporters of normalization argue that diplomatic relations could lead
to important improvements in bilateral relations. Over the next few
decades, the United States and China are unlikely to become major trading
partners, but in some economic sectors they could continue to complement
each other in significant ways. China clearly needs high-technology goods,
such as American petroleum exploration and drilling equipment, communications systems, computers, and metallurgical technology, while the
United States might become a consumer of substantial Chinese petroleum

exports. At the same time, the United States could follow the Peking-endorsed "Japanese formula," which permits extensive commercial relations with both the People's Republic and Taiwan. (This and other so-called formulas are discussed later.) In addition, normalization might lead to extended exchanges of students and scientists and to the creation of press bureaus in both countries, as it has for the Japanese, Western Europeans, and Canadians. Many proponents of normalization hold that such bilateral possibilities, taken in conjunction with other strategic and global considerations, make a cogent argument for diplomatic relations with Peking.

Impact on USSR and Japan

A third question concerns the possible impact of Sino-American diplomatic relations on the other major powers in Asia—the Soviet Union and Japan.

Opponents of normalization, as noted, hold that the Peking-Moscow-Washington strategic triangle has been a key determinant of Sino-American détente and that diplomatic relations with China are unlikely to make much difference to this triangle. Peking, obsessed with the threat from the Soviets on the northern border and Soviet expansionism elsewhere in Asia, badly needed American rapprochement as a counterweight to the "polar bear." As long as the Chinese see the Soviets as a threat and respect American military might, Sino-American détente probably will persist. If the threat diminishes or American military credibility weakens, then détente will be jeopardized. For the same reason, Peking has strongly endorsed the U.S.-Japan alliance; that alliance helps counteract Soviet pressure while it perpetuates the Japanese role as a prosperous economic power without nuclear or other offensive military weaponry. Sino-Japanese relations were enhanced dramatically in 1978 by the signing of an 8-year commercial pact and a treaty of peace and friendship.

Many supporters of normalization accept these strategic arguments but also urge the United States to look toward other great power relationships in Asia in which Sino-American diplomatic relations could be a significant factor. They see the emergence of a new era of "four-power politics" in Asia involving Japan, the Soviet Union, the United States, and the People's Republic of China. In this view, the balance of power among the four nations tends to inhibit military confrontation, and it could promote diplomatic, economic, and arms control negotiations among them. Indeed, the process has already begun in the 1970s; there have been significant negotiations on commercial matters involving these four powers in various triangular configurations. The Sino-American relationship is a missing diplomatic link; the Sino-Soviet relationship, a missing strategic link. Were these links established, the four powers might anticipate quadrilateral negotiations in future years bearing great implications for stability in Asia.

Such a situation is not certain, but it is a reasonable prospect, and a striking contrast to the past century in which all four powers have been involved in wars and confrontations.

Indeed, such a negotiations strategy might be applied to other key concerns in Asia, particularly the oil-rich areas of the East Asian continental shelf. In all these matters, the United States should operate in close consultation with its closest Asian ally, Japan, and avoid a repeat of the "Nixon shocks" of the early 1970s.

Impact on Taiwan and Korea

A fourth question concerns the possible impact of Sino-American normalization on various other nations in Asia.

Opponents hold that American withdrawal of recognition of Taiwan and abrogation of the mutual security treaty would constitute yet another blow to American credibility overseas. Its immediate impact on Taiwan is uncertain, but a worst-case argument envisions economic panic in Taiwan, the flight of capital and people from the island, a severe drop in Taiwan's trade, and an economic blockade or even military invasion by the mainland Chinese. Even if the worst case is avoided, the ripple effect on other Asian countries, particularly South Korea and Japan, might be serious. North Korea, emboldened by the weakened American commitment to treaty obligations, might launch an attack on South Korea, which might cause Communist Chinese and Russian involvement and leave the President and Congress with the terrible decision of whether to engage in another land war in Asia. Hostilities in Korea or economic panic in Taiwan would surely have substantial repercussions and might even lead to remilitarization in Japan. In quest of an embassy, the Pacific might be lost.

Supporters of normalization, the more sober among them at least, believe that any normalization agreement should provide reasonable protection for the commerce and security of Taiwan. With such safeguards, they believe it highly unlikely that Taiwan will suffer economic collapse and that China would risk the loss of life, military equipment, and prestige, as well as war with the United States, by attacking the island.

As for Korea, they agree that the peninsula is one of the most dangerous flashpoints in the world and support President Carter's intention to conduct a phased withdrawal of American ground troops. They also support eventual multilateral negotiations about Korea involving the four major powers as well as both Koreas. Once again, normalization would seem a prerequisite to the joint Sino-American involvement in such negotiations, since Peking is unwilling to discuss the Korean issue in detail under our current relationship.

In short, serious proponents of normalization recognize that there are risks in the policy they advocate, but believe that those risks can be minimized and that there are more serious risks in not normalizing relations with Peking. They also point to the long-term possiblities in Sino-American relations should the United States pursue an interlocking set of bilateral, regional, and strategic goals.

Impact on Global Problems

The final question concerns the effect of normalizing relations in promoting greater Chinese participation in international negotiations on major global issues, such as arms control, energy resources, and food supplies.

At present, the People's Republic participates in a number of international bodies, including the United Nations and the World Health Organization, but has remained aloof from others. Opponents and supporters of normalization agree that the People's Republic is unlikely to take part in more deliberative bodies in the near future and that diplomatic recognition is unlikely to have much immediate effect in this respect. Some advocates of recognition, however, believe that the long-term effects of Sino-American relations might encourage Chinese involvement in population and food questions, where the Chinese experience could be instructive for other parts of the globe, and in arms control, where China has as much at stake as other nuclear powers. The growing American commitment to including global interdependence as a factor in negotiations might carry weight with China if the two countries had normal relations. Opponents of recognition, on the other hand, argue that China will continue to act out of self-interest and that there is very little that the United States can do to promote a different Chinese approach to global problems.

Presidential Leadership

Clearly, there is no set of China policies that will win unanimous support from Congress, from other opinion leaders, and from the public at large. The opinion poll reported in this book offers some broad indications of the policies toward China most favored by the American public. But in looking back over the past century, it seems clear that the single most important influence in determining the American outlooks on China and Asia generally has been the President himself. The controversies surrounding foreign policy issues, and also the decisive role of presidential leadership, were demonstrated clearly in the Panama Canal Treaty debate.

The task of the President, whether he sides with the opponents or proponents of normalization, is to articulate a China policy which examines the issues on several levels and which best suits his overall view of American international interests. It is only in that broad context that he can make a persuasive case on the Taiwan issue, the most pressing bilateral problem facing Washington and Peking.

The Taiwan Issue

History

Taiwan became an issue between the United States and the People's Republic of China because of the Korean war. Roosevelt, Churchill, and Chiang Kai-shek had agreed at Cairo in 1943 that Taiwan would be taken from Japan, whose colony it had been since 1895, and returned to China. Accordingly, after Japan's defeat the government of the Republic of China took over the island. With the conquest of the China mainland by the Chinese Communists in 1949-1950, Taiwan became the last redoubt for Chiang Kai-shek and some 2 million civilian and military refugees from the mainland.

Early in 1950, President Truman, seeking to disengage the United States from entanglement in the Chinese civil war, declared:

> The United States has no desire to obtain special rights or privileges or to establish military bases on Formosa [Taiwan] at this time. Nor does it have any intention of utilizing its armed forces to interfere in the present situation. The United States Government will not pursue a course which will lead to involvement in the civil conflict in China. Similarly, the United States Government will not provide military aid or advice to Chinese forces on Formosa.

But with the outbreak of the Korean war in June 1950, the United States reversed its policy toward Taiwan overnight. President Truman stated:

> The occupation of Formosa by Communist forces would be a direct threat to the security of the Pacific area and to United States forces performing their lawful and necessary functions in that area. Accordingly, I have ordered the Seventh Fleet to prevent any attack on Formosa. . . . The determination of the future status of Formosa must await the restoration of security in the Pacific, a peace treaty with Japan, or consideration by the United Nations.

The unexpected attack on South Korea by the North Koreans came only a few months after the newly established government of the People's Republic of China had signed a 30-year treaty of alliance with the Soviet Union directed against Japan and the United States. This resort to force by North Korea, with the backing of the USSR and China, convinced U.S.

authorities that it would be prudent to deny Taiwan to the PRC, at least for the time being, and to lift the self-imposed ban on military and economic aid to the Republic of China on Taiwan.

By the end of the Korean war, Americans and mainland Chinese had come to regard each other as enemies, and there was little inclination in the United States to terminate aid to Taiwan and revert to neutrality toward the two sides in the civil war. During the next 20 years a complex network of relations grew up between the United States and Taiwan.

The mutual defense treaty signed in 1954 made the Republic of China on Taiwan a link in the chain of defense pacts from Japan and South Korea to Australia and New Zealand concluded by the United States principally to prevent the expansion of Soviet and Chinese Communist power in Asia. Some $3.5 billion in U.S. military aid and the training of thousands of military personnel in the United States contributed to the creation of a modern military force in Taiwan.

Another $3.2 billion in economic aid helped to stabilize Taiwan's economy and build the base for rapid, self-sustaining growth. American businessmen began to invest in Taiwan, and trade between the two countries flourished. American missionaries and educators, denied access to mainland China, shifted their activities to Taiwan. Thousands of graduates of universities in Taiwan came to the United States for advanced study. A small number returned to Taiwan; most remained in the United States as permanent residents or became American citizens. By the time President Nixon made his historic trip to Peking in 1972, a great number of ties, official and private, had developed between the United States and Taiwan.

The People's Republic bitterly protested the decision by the United States to prevent the "liberation" of Taiwan. Lacking the military force to contest the decision, PRC authorities entered into ambassadorial-level talks with the United States in 1955, hoping to further their recognition as the legitimate government of China in the eyes of Washington and the United Nations and, ultimately, to acquire Taiwan. But the United States rejected PRC proposals to open trade and other relations between the two countries and continued to support the Republic of China as the legitimate government of China in the UN. It pressed the People's Republic without success to renounce the use of force in the Taiwan area.

In 1958 Mao Tse-tung, believing that the world balance of forces had shifted in favor of the Sino-Soviet bloc, decided to test the U.S. commitment to the defense of Taiwan by a massive artillery bombardment aimed at interdicting the resupply of the islands just off the China coast occupied by the ROC. The United States helped Taiwan break the attempted blockade, making it clear to Peking that the United States would not allow the island to fall into the PRC's hands. Although the United States then began to propose small steps to improve relations between the two countries, for the next

13 years the People's Republic held rigidly to the position that no improvement in relations with the United States could take place until the Taiwan problem had been resolved.

The formula arrived at in the Shanghai Communiqué required significant concessions by both parties. Peking dropped its insistence that the Taiwan problem be resolved before relations between Washington and Peking could be improved. Washington, while not explicitly repudiating the position it had taken in 1950, namely that the status of Taiwan was undetermined, declared that it did not challenge the view taken by the Chinese on the mainland and in Taiwan that Taiwan was part of China. In effect, Washington and Peking agreed that the Taiwan issue would be put to one side so as not to obstruct the improvement of relations between them. In addition, Washington expressed interest in a peaceful settlement of the Taiwan question by the Chinese themselves and pledged the ultimate withdrawal of all its military personnel and installations from the island. The Shanghai Communiqué laid down certain guidelines for the conduct of relations between the United States and the People's Republic, including the ultimate resolution of the Taiwan issue itself, but fell far short of resolving that issue.

Since release of the Shanghai Communiqué, the United States has substantially reduced its military presence on Taiwan, but in other respects its bonds with the island have become stronger. A U.S. trade center was opened in Taipei in 1973, and U.S. trade with Taiwan soared from $1.8 billion in 1972 to $5.6 billion in 1977—15 times the value of U.S. trade with the China mainland. U.S. Export-Import Bank loans and guarantees to Taiwan have reached nearly $2 billion. Private American investment now exceeds $500 million. American companies represented in the American Chamber of Commerce in Taipei increased from 60 in 1972 to 220 in 1977. Eight American banks maintain branches in Taiwan, and more than 5500 American civilians reside there. In 1972 the United States signed a 30-year agreement with the ROC undertaking to supply enriched uranium for the nuclear power plants under construction and those planned for the future. In 1974, the coproduction of F5E fighter aircraft began in Taiwan.

Thus, although the United States is no longer providing economic aid or large amounts of military aid, as it did in the 1950s and 1960s, its ties with Taiwan in the fields of advanced technology and economic and business interchange have increased.

Normalization Formulas and Taiwan

The establishment of full-fledged diplomatic relations between the United States and the People's Republic could, in theory, be accomplished in various ways.

At one extreme is the "German formula," so called because under it the United States would have diplomatic relations with both parts of China, just as it has with both parts of Germany. The United States would formally recognize the People's Republic as the sole legitimate government of China and exchange ambassadors with it, while maintaining relations with Taiwan, including embassies in the two capitals and the security treaty.

At the other extreme is the full and unconditional acceptance by the United States of the terms for normalization stated publicly by the People's Republic, ending diplomatic relations and the security treaty with Taiwan but continuing economic relations through nonofficial arrangements similar to those worked out between Japan and Taiwan after Tokyo and Peking normalized relations in 1972.

Other conceivable formulas lie between these two extremes. The United States might, for example, agree to some of but not all the People's Republic's terms. Or it might accept all those terms but insist on reciprocal assurances by the PRC that would reduce the threat to Taiwan.

A formula that would conform fully to the interests of the United States and the People's Republic is difficult to imagine. The United States would like to normalize on terms that accorded the people of Taiwan the largest feasible degree of freedom to decide their own future. The People's Republic would prefer terms that most weakened Taiwan's ability to resist future mainland pressures and inducements. An acceptable compromise will not be easy to reach. Both sides will have difficult judgments to make as to how much they value the improved international position resulting from normalization over the costs that would be incurred—by the United States in weakening its connections with Taiwan, and by the People's Republic in acquiescing to a continued U.S. relationship with Taiwan. Both also will have to decide whether the costs of failing to achieve normalization would outweigh the costs of accepting a less than satisfactory arrangement on Taiwan.

Taiwan's Fears. In considering what terms for normalization of relations might be acceptable, the United States will have to take account of the impact on Taiwan itself of the formula selected. The people of Taiwan want no change in their relations with the United States. They have prospered under the relationship that has existed for the past 25 years, during which Taiwan's economy and security have depended heavily on the U.S. connection. They fear that if Taiwan came under control of the People's Republic, their way of life would suffer radical change and their standard of living would fall to that on the mainland.

People in Taiwan are especially fearful that elimination of the security treaty and the withdrawal of U.S. military personnel would open the way for a military attack on Taiwan or an attempt to blockade the island's commerce—perhaps not immediately, but before many years had passed. Taiwan is not defenseless. It has a military force of 500,000 equipped with weapons roughly equivalent in quality to those possessed by the People's Republic. Moreover, it would be risky and difficult to land and maintain a force large enough to defeat the defenders across the more than 90 miles of ocean separating Taiwan from the mainland. The PRC today lacks the landing craft and other specialized equipment necessary to undertake with confidence so large an amphibious operation. Nevertheless, Taiwan's forces are heavily outnumbered in tanks, artillery, fighter aircraft, submarines, and missile-firing patrol crafts. The People's Republic also has bombers and nuclear-tipped missiles; Taiwan has no bombers and no nuclear weapons. ROC authorities fear that within a few years the PRC could acquire the amphibious capability it now lacks and could win a war of attrition, provided it were willing to take heavy losses and the United States did not intervene. They are also concerned that if the United States severed diplomatic relations and ended the security treaty, they no longer would have access to spare parts for their American equipment and to advanced weapons to replace those becoming obsolete.

Taiwan is also heavily dependent on the United States economically. Exports constitute 48 percent of its gross national product, and the United States buys 39 percent of these. As mentioned, Taiwan has received significant amounts of capital from the United States. This capital flow is important, not for its volume, since domestic capital now meets the great bulk of investment needs, but mainly to provide advanced technology and management and marketing skills. Most important of all is the confidence in the future of Taiwan which the American connection gives the entrepreneur, who is the mainstay of Taiwan's private enterprise economy. Authorities on Taiwan fear a flight of capital and people if the terms of U.S. normalization with the People's Republic substantially impair existing relations between Taiwan and the United States.

The government of the Republic of China does have other possible means of seeking to safeguard its security and prosperity than its connection with the United States. It could, for example, abandon its "one China" position and declare Taiwan an independent state. American recognition of the new state would create severe strain between Peking and Washington. Peking has adamantly opposed a "two Chinas" or "one China, one Taiwan" arrangement and would regard U.S. support for an independent Taiwan as a violation of the U.S. position enunciated in the Shanghai Communiqué, which President Carter has pledged to uphold. On the other hand, there would be widespread sympathy among Americans for the right of the 17 million people of Taiwan to self-determination.

Another possible option for Taiwan is the production of nuclear weapons. Although the Republic of China is a signatory of the nuclear

nonproliferation treaty and has publicly stated it will not manufacture
nuclear weapons, it has the technical capabilities and could do so within a
few years if it felt sufficiently threatened.

Still another option is to develop a relationship with the USSR. Neither
Moscow nor Taipei seems inclined to move in this direction, but it is not difficult to imagine circumstances—especially should the People's Republic
become more hostile or the United States less friendly—under which both
parties might see advantages in it.

From the ROC viewpoint, a continued, strong connection with the
United States is far more desirable than any of the above options. ROC
leaders are not likely to adopt any of them, except in desperation. Yet the
existence of the options must be kept in mind by the United States and the
People's Republic as they consider terms for normalization.

Impact on Japan. The United States also must concern itself with the impact on Japan of the formula selected for normalization. Maintenance of
close and cordial relations with Japan is a vital U.S. interest, one accorded a
high priority by the Carter administration. Having themselves normalized
relations with the PRC, the Japanese do not object in principle to the
United States doing the same. But they hope that it will be done with care so
as not to disturb unduly Taiwan and Japan's important relations with the
island.

The "German Formula." Of the various conceivable formulas for nor-
malization, the "German formula" would be the easiest for the United
States, Japan, and Taiwan to accept, because it would require no change in
U.S. relations with Taiwan. Although the ROC would protest the establishment of ambassadorial relations between the United States and the People's
Republic, it would not sever relations with the United States over the issue.
But Peking has made it abundantly clear that it would reject this formula.
PRC leaders could not afford to agree to a formalized "two Chinas" ar-
rangement which required not only a retreat from the understanding
reached with the United States in the Shanghai Communiqué but also the
abandonment of their plans for the ultimate "liberation" of Taiwan.

Despite the certainty of Peking's rejection, the United States still might
make the proposal in the hope that after a number of years Peking might
agree to it. After all, after many years of holding tenaciously to its position,
Peking finally dropped its insistence on the resolution of the Taiwan problem as a precondition for the improvement of relations with the United
States. But if the United States were to insist on the German formula, it
would have to be prepared for a deterioration of relations with the People's
Republic, perhaps for a long time. Chinese and Soviet advocates of improved
relations between the two communist powers would be much encouraged.

The risk would increase that the United States and the People's Republic might slip back into a condition of outspoken hostility and even military confrontation. The administration would be subjected to considerable criticism for having adopted a rigid and unproductive approach to normalization.

The "Japanese Formula." What about the "Japanese formula," which officials in Peking have indicated privately would be acceptable to them? This would require the United States to break diplomatic relations with Taiwan and end the security treaty, but would permit the establishment in Taipei and Washington of "unofficial" missions staffed by foreign service officers of the two countries "on leave" from the State Department and Foreign Ministry. It would permit the continuance of trade and investment.

The trouble with the Japanese formula is that it makes no provision for Taiwan's security. The United States has had a formal commitment for over 20 years to assist in the defense of Taiwan, while Japan had no such responsibility. Consequently, the Japanese formula falls short of meeting U.S. needs. President Carter has said publicly that the United States does not want to see the people of Taiwan "punished or attacked." Secretary of State Vance has said that the security of the people of Taiwan "is essential" to the United States. If the United States were to agree to Peking's conditions without taking steps to safeguard Taiwan's security, Tokyo, Taipei, and many Americans would be shocked.

An "American Formula." What seems to be needed is an "American formula" that would protect U.S. relations with Taiwan, yet not foreclose the possibility of a peaceful, negotiated settlement of the Taiwan issue sometime in the future by the Chinese on the mainland and on Taiwan. If the United States agrees to terminate diplomatic relations and the security treaty with Taiwan, it will be making substantial concessions, for which it should be possible to insist on reciprocal concessions from the People's Republic that would preserve the substance of U.S. relations with Taiwan. Such U.S. concessions would be significant, not only because of the stress placed on them by the People's Republic, but also because, once taken, they would be difficult to reverse. Reciprocal concessions from the People's Republic are needed with respect to U.S. economic and security ties with Taiwan.

Informal indications that the People's Republic would not object to economic relations between the United States and Taiwan similar to those between Japan and Taiwan suggest that agreement in this area may not be too difficult. But U.S.-Taiwanese economic relations are more dependent on government-to-government agreements than were those between Japan and Taiwan.

Japan took the view that severance of diplomatic relations terminated all official agreements with Taiwan. Similar action by the United States would severely damage economic relations with Taiwan unless unofficial agreements of some kind promptly replaced the official agreements. It is doubtful, however, whether under U.S. law the official agreements could be effectively replaced by unofficial ones, similar to those worked out by the Japanese. U.S. economic agreements with Taiwan include the Treaty of Friendship and Commerce, which gives Taiwan's exports to the United States most-favored-nation treatment; an agreement on the supply of enriched uranium for Taiwan's power industry; an agreement under which the Overseas Private Investment Corporation guarantees American private investment in Taiwan; agreements on quotas for the export of textiles and shoes to the United States; and loan agreements of the Export-Import Bank. Those agreements essential to the continuance of economic relations between the United States and Taiwan could be kept in force by an act of Congress.

Some form of official or quasi-official U.S. representation on Taiwan also would be needed to manage the continuing relations between Washington and Taipei. Secretary Vance proposed to Vice Premier Teng Hsiao-p'ing in August 1977 that a U.S. embassy be established in Peking and a liaison office in Taipei, thus reversing Washington's present diplomatic relationships with the two parts of China; but Teng rejected this proposal on the ground that it would preserve diplomatic relations between the United States and Taiwan. Possible substitutes for diplomatic relations include consular relations, trade missions, or ostensibly private organizations similar to those established to manage relations between Japan and Taiwan.

Future security relations between the United States and Taiwan will pose a more difficult problem for Washington and Peking in the negotiations on normalization than will future economic relations. Even if Washington were to comply with Peking's demand for an end to the security treaty with Taipei as a condition of normalization, it would continue to be concerned about Taiwan's security, as President Carter and Secretary Vance have made clear. Of course, as long as the People's Republic needs satisfactory relations with the United States and Japan, it will be inhibited from using military force against Taiwan. But Washington would not wish to rely on these circumstances continuing indefinitely. At the very least, Washington would wish to permit the ROC to continue to buy spare parts for its American equipment. It probably would want to be in a position to sell more advanced weapons systems to Taiwan as Taiwan's present equipment becomes obsolete. It also would want assurance that Peking envisaged a peaceful resolution of the Taiwan problem—an assurance Peking has refused to give publicly and, many observers agree, is unlikely to give in the future. Washington, in addition, would warn Peking that use of force against Taiwan would gravely damage Sino-American relations.

Thus negotiations on normalization present difficulties for both parties. The United States will find it hard to make immediate, concrete concessions for potentially important, long-run benefits that are both intangible and uncertain. The Carter administration must obtain from Peking credible assurances that U.S. relations with Taiwan will not be seriously jeopardized. Otherwise, its actions would be difficult to defend before American critics. But it will be hard for Peking to provide credible assurances that existing substantive relations between the United States and this portion of Chinese territory can continue, even though the United States agrees to change the form of those relations. Leaders in Peking doubtless are constrained by the risk of making what their political opponents might seize upon as concessions of principle to the United States in regard to China's sovereign rights.

Of course, both parties have a strong motivation—concern about the USSR—not to allow the Taiwan issue to block improvement in their relations. They also have a common interest in avoiding the kind of pressure on Taiwan that might drive it to develop nuclear weapons or to seek a connection with the USSR. Consequently, they may be able to work out a reasonable compromise or, failing that, agree to postpone negotiations to a more propitious time without allowing the delay to lead to a deterioration of bilateral relations. But both sides probably recognize that prolonged delay would be risky, for there is no assurance that the passage of time will make normalization easier to accomplish; indeed, the loss of forward momentum in the last few years suggests the reverse.

8   American Perceptions

In mid-April 1977 a special survey of American attitudes toward the People's Republic of China and Taiwan was undertaken by Potomac Associates. The results can be summarized as follows.

Overall, the American people view Taiwan considerably more favorably than they do mainland China. The prospective emergence of the People's Republic as a major world power is a development that our citizens do not see as in the best interests of the United States. Nor do Americans want to interfere in the Sino-Soviet dispute by enhancing Peking's military capabilities vis-à-vis Moscow.

The question of full diplomatic recognition of the People's Republic puts Americans in a quandary. In the abstract, they are clearly in favor of such a move. But when Peking's preconditions for this step are introduced—severance of our diplomatic and military links with Taiwan—Americans do a complete about-face. Even on the condition that the President give assurances of continued U.S. interest in the security of the people of Taiwan, a substantial plurality of Americans oppose resumption of diplomatic relations on Peking's terms.

This concern for Taiwan does not mean, however, that Americans are keen on committing themselves to Taiwan's defense should it come under attack from the mainland. On that subject, Americans are very split in their views, with more opposed to such a U.S. involvement than in favor.

Before discussing these findings in detail, let us first set the stage by reviewing earlier opinion research on these and related issues.

Unfortunately, a good deal of available data is not pertinent to this study. To begin, much of the information concerns the admission of the People's Republic to the United Nations, once a burning issue but now passé. Also, a number of previous surveys questioned very small sample groups or were undertaken by organizations with a particular interest in the outcome; in the latter, use of biased terminology may have influenced responses. Little weight will be given to either of these types of surveys.

Here, then, are the highlights of some especially useful studies undertaken in recent years, broken down by subject area.

General Impressions of China and the Chinese

Popularity

The contrasting levels of popularity of mainland China as against Taiwan that emerge in our 1977 survey continue a long-term trend. In 1967, for example, the Gallup Organization surveyed Americans to measure levels of like or dislike toward a number of countries. Next to the United States, Canada received the most positive rating (94 percent favorable). Lowest of all at that time was the People's Republic (identified in the survey as "Communist China"), with only 5 percent favorable. Taiwan was not included in the 1967 survey.

In 1972, in the aftermath of President Nixon's journey to Peking, Gallup repeated its overall rating question, this time asking about both the People's Republic (again identified as Communist China) and the Republic of China (identified as Nationalist China/Taiwan). The results showed a sharp rise in favorable views of the People's Republic—up to 23 percent positive. Taiwan fared far better in the eyes of Americans, however, with 55 percent of those surveyed registering positive views.

Gallup continued its periodic testing of overall attitudes toward a number of countries in September 1975, this time under contract to the Republic of China (ROC) in Taiwan. The wording was essentially the same as in other Gallup surveys in this series, making the results fully comparable. In the fall of 1975, as cultural exchanges and other visits between the People's Republic and the United States grew, 28 percent expressed favorable views toward the PRC, 48 percent toward the Republic of China on Taiwan. This represented a net shift of 12 points away from Taiwan toward the mainland.

The most recent Gallup survey of this kind was carried out in September 1976. As the pace of developments between Washington and Peking slowed, and since leadership changes in the PRC may have put the mainland in a more uncertain light in American eyes, there was a shift back in favor of Taiwan at the expense of the People's Republic: 55 percent were favorable to the island and 20 percent favorable to the mainland, a net gain over the previous year of 15 points for Taiwan. The results were very close to those recorded in 1972. By a margin of nearly 3 to 1, Americans were more favorably disposed toward Taiwan than the People's Republic.

Power and Importance

Another way of measuring the views of Americans about other countries is in terms of overall power and importance. This method was employed by

Potomac Associates in 1974 and 1976, when a national cross section of citizens was asked to rate the "power and importance" of various countries on a ladder with steps ranging from 0 at the bottom (representing a very small, weak power) to 10 at the top (denoting a very great power). In the 1974 survey people also were asked to rate where the United States had stood 10 years in the past and where they would expect it to be 10 years in the future. For other countries, people were asked only about the present and future. The rankings of the United States, the Soviet Union, and the People's Republic in 1974 were as follows ("n/a" indicates "not asked"):

	Past	*Present*	*Future*
The United States	9.2	8.8	8.0
The Soviet Union	n/a	7.8	7.9
The People's Republic of China	n/a	6.0	6.8

The public consensus in 1974 was that the United States still had significantly greater power and importance than the Soviet Union. The future ratings of the two nations, however, were virtually identical. (To be statistically significant, a difference in ratings must amount to at least 0.6 step of the ladder.) Americans, in other words, saw a state of equivalence looming up in 10 years as their country's power and importance declined while the Soviet Union held its own.

In the case of mainland China, Americans in 1974 anticipated a significant increase in overall power and importance over the next 10 years. Although the People's Republic was expected to continue to rank well behind the two superpowers, the fact should be underscored that, unlike the United States and the Soviet Union, China was seen as a nation on the move.

The 1976 power and importance ratings—this time for the past, present, and future in all three countries—showed a major change in the public's assessment:

	Past	*Present*	*Future*
The United States	8.9	8.5	8.4
The Soviet Union	6.9	8.2	8.6
The People's Republic of China	4.7	6.6	7.7

In comparing the United States and the Soviet Union first, the difference in respective present and future ratings for both countries was less than 0.6 step of the ladder, meaning no appreciable change in power and importance was foreseen for either nation over the next 10 years. And the belief in future equivalence held three years ago remained. In contrast to their view of the situation in 1974, however, Americans in 1976 concluded that the Soviet Union at present was virtually the equal of the United States. Americans saw the Soviet Union as having grown rapidly in power and importance, advancing more than one full step on the ladder (from 6.9 to 8.2) during the past 10 years. As in 1974, Americans believed the United States had lost ground in the previous decade, although not enough to be statistically significant.

The 1976 ratings of mainland China, on the other hand, although as in 1974 lower than those for the United States and the Soviet Union, showed a much more dynamic pattern. Americans perceived China as having risen almost two full steps on the ladder over the last decade. And, as in 1974, they foresaw an increase in the power and importance of China over the next 10 years, while those of the United States and the Soviet Union leveled off. Experts may doubt whether China will approach the level of the Soviet Union and the United States by the mid-1980s in the traditional measurements of power. The public's interpretation of overall power and importance of a nation, however, can take into account a number of factors other than comparative military and economic standing. Given China's size, population, and influence in many fields, the relatively high and sharply ascending ratings given China by Americans have much to support them.

Views on Recognition and Diplomatic Relations

A landmark study on American attitudes toward China was undertaken by the University of Michigan's Survey Research Center in mid-1964. Among the key findings was the fact that 51 percent of those questioned favored "exchanging ambassadors with Communist China the way we do with other countries"; 34 percent opposed such a step.

Eleven years later, in the 1975 Gallup survey taken on behalf of Taiwan, 61 percent favored "establishing diplomatic relations with the People's Republic of China—Mainland China," while 23 percent were opposed. At the same time, however, Americans favored continued formal relations with "Nationalist China on Taiwan" by a margin of 70 to 14 percent. Furthermore, only 10 percent felt that the United States should withdraw recognition from Nationalist China in order to establish relations with the "People's Republic of China," and 70 percent thought the United States should not do this.

In early 1977 the Foreign Policy Association tabulated approximately 5000 ballots received on the China issue in its annual nationwide foreign policy discussion program. Among this group, whose members have a far greater than average interest in foreign affairs and the international arena,

33 percent were willing to accept Peking's preconditions—severance of U.S. diplomatic and military ties with Taiwan—as the cost of normalization of our relations, while 53 percent were opposed. Support jumped sharply—to 74 percent in favor and only 14 percent opposed—if Peking were prepared to give "firm assurances" it would use only peaceful means to resolve the status of Taiwan. Almost the same proportion favored the status quo when it was offered as another alternative: 69 percent wanted to continue present policies (defined as "maintain full diplomatic relations with Taiwan; liaison office in Peking; defense treaty with Taiwan; encourage trade with both"), while 19 percent were opposed.

That Peking's preconditions pose a vexing question and that Americans are reluctant to sacrifice Taiwan are clear from these responses. We return to these matters in greater detail when we turn to the results of our April 1977 survey.

Attitudes on Military Issues

The dichotomy inherent in the views of Americans about the two claimants to power in China is particularly evident when the question arises of the United States coming to the defense of Taiwan in the event of attack.

In an April 1971 Potomac Associates survey, for example, only 11 percent of Americans favored sending U.S. troops to defend "Nationalist China in the event [it] is attacked by communist-backed forces." An additional 30 percent favored sending military supplies only and not American troops, while 45 percent wanted no involvement.

Gallup repeated this question in April 1975 and found an even more cautious outlook: only 8 percent were prepared to commit U.S. troops and 27 percent supplies, while 54 percent wanted no involvement.

Prior to the second of these surveys, Louis Harris and Associates found, in a study in December 1974, that 17 percent of the public and 11 percent of a special sample of individuals selected as experts in international affairs would favor U.S. military involvement, including the use of U.S. troops, in the event "Communist China invaded Formosa [Taiwan]"; 59 percent of the public and 79 percent of the expert group were opposed. The results of this survey are not directly comparable with the Potomac Associates and Gallup studies that came before and after it, since Harris provided essentially two options, and the others provided three. By postulating the use of U.S. troops as the only means of intervention, Harris recorded an increase in the percentage of those in favor of noninvolvement.

The commitment of U.S. forces is of obvious concern to many Americans. In the October 1975 survey undertaken by Gallup for the ROC discussed earlier, for example, Americans were far more sympathetic to a

proposition that put the U.S. commitment in abstract terms, without defin-
ing the precise nature of potential involvement. Thus, when this question
was asked—"We now have a mutual defense treaty with Nationalist China,
approved by Congress in 1954. Do you think the United States should continue to stand by this treaty to defend Nationalist China in the event of an
attack?"—47 percent of those interviewed said yes and 31 percent no.
When respondents are reminded of the treaty obligation and the price is not
spelled out, Americans apparently find it easier to support a commitment to
stand by allies.

Attitudes toward China and the Chinese

Having looked briefly at some earlier survey data on the attitudes of
Americans toward mainland China and Taiwan, let us now turn to the
special survey undertaken by Potomac Associates.

The survey was conducted over the weekend of April 16-17, 1977, a time
when no major events in U.S.-Chinese relations were occurring. In the
absence of any particular media coverage of questions pertaining to China,
the public presumably was not being stirred or motivated one way or
another in its immediate reactions to the questions.

The survey started with a number of questions designed to test levels of
awareness about China—both the People's Republic of China on the
mainland and the Republic of China on Taiwan—and the overall attitudes
of Americans toward the two claimants to power.

Ideological Cast

The opening questions were informational—what do Americans know
about the ideological makeup of the governments in Peking and Taipei?

> *As you probably know, for many years two rival governments have
> called themselves China: On the one hand, the People's Republic or
> Mainland China on the continent of Asia, and, on the other hand, the
> Republic of China on the island of Taiwan (or Formosa, as it is
> sometimes called). Do you happen to know, does the Republic of China
> on Taiwan have a communist government or not?*

Yes, it does	17%
No, it does not	44
Don't know	39

> *And does Mainland China have a communist government or not?*

Yes, it does	67%
No, it does not	4
Don't know	29

The American people are moderately well informed about the coloration of the regime in Peking. Two-thirds (67 percent) know it is communist, and this figure rises to 86 percent among the college-educated. Yet after all the years since the accession to power of Mao and his colleagues in 1949 and the experience of the Korean and Vietnam wars, the fact remains that one-third of the American public is misinformed about the ideological makeup of the Peking government.

Knowledge about Taiwan's government is of an even far lower order. If we combine those who say it is communist and those who don't know, a majority (56 percent) are either misinformed or uninformed. Those most knowledgeable on this issue include men (54 percent of whom are aware that the government of the Republic of China is not communist, whereas only 34 percent of women know this), those with a college education (69 percent know it is not communist), and residents of the West, where geographic proximity probably plays a role (57 percent say it is not communist).

Given the extensive coverage of things Chinese in the U.S. press and on radio and television, especially in the years since Nixon's 1972 visit to Peking, this represents a heavy load of misinformation about Taiwan. To be sure, the conflicting claims of Peking and Taipei against each other contribute a degree of confusion to the whole issue. Still this is one of many examples found in survey research of the low level of awareness of Americans about the specifics of foreign policy. In *American Public Opinion and U.S. Foreign Policy 1975*, a report by the Chicago Council on Foreign Relations based on research conducted by Louis Harris and Associates, it was stated that "no more than 31 percent of the public sampled followed any foreign news event closely, and the highest rating in the December 1974 sample tended to go to events then in prominence. On average, only about 20 percent of the public follows foreign policy issues very closely."

This fact holds important policy implications for the Carter administration. Throughout our 1977 survey on China, even on questions of attitude rather than of awareness or knowledge, the number of Americans who "don't know" is consistently rather large. Such high levels of uncertainty or ignorance tend to give the President considerable room for maneuver and, should he so desire, a major opportunity for public education. The many Americans who are not vitally concerned with developments beyond their borders are not likely to stand in the way of vigorous presidential action, as long as those actions seem reasonable and within general perceptions of the national interest.

General Attitudes

It will be recalled from chapter 1 that attitudes toward the two parts of China differed considerably in the 1977 survey. On a favorable/unfavorable basis, and including results from the 1978 survey as well, Taiwan ranked second behind Japan, followed by South Korea, the People's Republic, and North Korea.

By a 2-to-1 margin, 52 to 26 percent, Americans hold negative as opposed to positive views toward the People's Republic. But they lean in Taiwan's favor, and by a 3-to-1 margin: 56 percent hold either "very" or "somewhat" favorable opinions, while only 18 percent maintain negative sentiments. These contrasting views, as we shall see shortly, are paralleled by answers to the question of possible full diplomatic recognition of Peking at the expense of ceasing to recognize Taipei.

Among various groups within the sample, those with a college education are somewhat more favorable toward the mainland: 37 percent are positive, 11 points above the average. The college-educated are also slightly more positive than the norm in their views toward Taiwan (63 percent favorable, compared with 56 percent for the sample as a whole), although the margin is just at the edge of statistical reliability.

Political affiliation does not play a major role in this question, particularly as concerns mainland China. Among both Republicans and Democrats one in four (24 percent) is "very" or "somewhat" favorable toward mainland China; 30 percent of Independents feel this way. On the unfavorable side are 58 percent of Republicans, 52 percent of Democrats, and 48 percent of Independents.

As to Taiwan, Democrats are slightly more reserved: 53 percent are favorable, compared to 58 percent of Independents, and 62 percent of Republicans. In the cases of both countries, the differences between Democrats and Republicans are not of major proportions, and their views largely conform to the national figures.

Attitudes toward the Mainland's Emerging Power

As discussed earlier, Americans perceive the People's Republic of China as a nation on the move, gaining rapidly in importance and power on both the United States and the Soviet Union. This is not a development that the public views with equanimity, however; nor do citizens favor U.S. intervention in the Sino-Soviet dispute by providing military support to China. Two questions in our survey raised these matters:

Mainland China has said it wants to develop economically and become a major power by the year 2000. Do you think it would be in the best interests of the United States for mainland China to become a great power by the year 2000?

Would be	18%
Would not be	58
Don't know	24

Mainland China is anxious to prevent the increase of Soviet power and influence in Asia and other parts of the world. Although we have fundamental political and ideological differences with mainland China, do you think the United States should help China build up its military strength to resist Soviet power and influence, or should we not help China in this way?

Assist China	11%
Not help China	70
Don't know	19

Nearly six Americans in ten sense the emergence of mainland China as a major power to be a development unfavorable to U.S. interests. Part of the explanation for this probably lies in the reasonable feeling that one adversary in the superpower class is enough.

This uneasiness about the prospect of the People's Republic playing an expanded power role in the world clearly comes into play when consideration is given to helping China enhance its military capability vis-à-vis the Soviet Union. Seven Americans in ten (70 percent) oppose such a move on our part, and the proportion rises to almost eight in ten (79 percent) among the college-educated. Trying to manipulate the triangular Washington-Moscow-Peking relationship and exploit the Sino-Soviet rift through military-related assistance is overwhelmingly rejected. As recent Potomac Associates research elsewhere demonstrates, Americans are increasingly cautious about undertaking new commitments or involvements abroad.[1] Reluctance to support Peking against Moscow in a quasi-military fashion is but one more sign of that outlook. (One is also tempted to speculate that this also indicates an aversion to arms sales in general, but the data on their own do not warrant that inference.)

Attitudes on Diplomatic Recognition

Against this background, let us now turn to the heart of the 1977 findings—the interrelated issues of possible recognition of the People's Republic and breaking of relations with Taiwan, and defense of the latter should it come under attack by the People's Republic.

In an abstract sense, Americans are clearly in favor of establishing full diplomatic relations with the People's Republic:

The two rival Chinese governments insist that the U.S. can have formal diplomatic relations with only one of them. The U.S. has had diplomatic relations and a defense pact with the Republic of China on Taiwan for many years. The U.S. still has only limited relationships with mainland China and is the only major country in the world without an embassy there. How important do you, yourself, think it is for the U.S. to establish full diplomatic relations and exchange ambassadors with mainland China—very important, fairly important, not particularly important, or not important at all?

Very important	31%
Fairly important	31
Not particularly important	13
Not important at all	8
Don't know	17

Of the sample 62 percent believe it is very or fairly important that the United States exchange ambassadors with mainland China; less than one American in twelve (8 percent) thinks such a move is not important at all. The college-educated, who constitute one of the most influential demographic groups in American society, are the most favorable of all on this point: 75 percent think full recognition is either fairly or very important.

Once again, party affiliation is not a significant variable: among Republicans, 63 percent support recognition in principle, as do 58 percent of Democrats and 68 percent of Independents.

This distinctly favorable view of full relations undergoes a dramatic reversal, however, when Peking's public preconditions—an end to U.S. diplomatic and military ties with Taiwan—are brought forward:

Mainland China has said it will establish diplomatic relations with the United States only if the U.S. ends its present diplomatic and defense treaty relations with Taiwan, but mainland China has indicated that it has no objections to our continuing economic ties with Taiwan. Suppose that in order to establish diplomatic relations with mainland China, President Carter urges that we end diplomatic and defense treaty relations with Taiwan while at the same time we continue our interest in the security of the people of Taiwan. Would you be very strongly in favor, fairly strongly in favor, fairly strongly opposed, or very strongly opposed?

Very strongly in favor	8%
Fairly strongly in favor	20
Fairly strongly opposed	25
Very strongly opposed	22
Don't know	25

What had been a 62-to-21 percent favorable balance toward full and formal diplomatic links with Peking now becomes 47-to-28 percent opposition, even if those links are conditioned with a presidential expression of continued U.S. interest in the "security of the people of Taiwan." This turnabout is all the more striking when account is taken of the extreme ends of the spectrum: those very strongly opposed outnumber those very strongly in favor by a margin of almost 3-to-1 (22 to 8 percent).

Views among the college-educated are again the most striking deviation from the norm. Because relatively few of them are undecided (13 percent), college graduates are both marginally more in favor (31 percent, as against the national average of 28 percent) and significantly more opposed (56 percent, compared with 47 percent for the nation as a whole).

Political affiliation has no particular bearing on this issue: Republicans, Democrats, and Independents all line up close to the national figures.

On this question, respondents also were given the opportunity to express in their own words why they answer as they do—why they favor or oppose establishing formal diplomatic ties with Peking on Peking's terms while maintaining American interest in the security of the people on Taiwan. The responses volunteered to this question are as follows:[b]

Favorable:

We should all live together in peace.	8%
We should have better relations with China; beneficial to us.	7
China's size demands recognition.	6
Taiwan is not worth the trouble.	3
If the president and our government decided to go ahead, we trust their judgment.	2
Taiwan is corrupt.	1

Unfavorable:

We should not turn our backs on friends.	29
Mainland China is communist.	10
We should trade with both; be friends with both.	9
U.S. should not succumb to foreign pressures.	6
We should stay out; don't get involved.	5
Mainland China is strong and a danger to us.	4
Don't trust Chinese.	3

Miscellaneous	6
Don't know.	16

One overriding conclusion leaps forward from these statements. Whereas no single factor stands out among the favorable comments, a very important, emotion-laden theme is by far the chief reason for not going along with Peking's conditions, even with the caveat about the security of

---

[b]The totals do not add up to the percentage of "favorable" and "unfavorable" because individuals could give more than one reason for their position.

Taiwan: almost three Americans in ten volunteer the view that we should not turn our backs on friends. This is clearly the kind of theme around which opposition to Peking's formula can cluster, in considerably greater numbers than exist now. It is something that President Carter and his advisers must take into account. While one can argue that Americans might be satisfied that their concerns on this issue have been met were adequate assurances on Taiwan negotiated, it is at least equally plain that the prospect of an American pullout that would sacrifice an old friend and ally could become the touchstone for emotional reactions in many quarters. One can almost imagine a new debate reminiscent of the "who lost China?" imbroglio of some three decades ago.

Attitudes on Taiwan's Security

That Taiwan is the critical issue that turns Americans against recognizing Peking on its terms is underscored by another question posed in the new survey:

Specifically, in considering the possibility of establishing diplomatic relations with mainland China, how important is it to you personally that the United States continue our interest in the security of the people of Taiwan?

Very important	30%
Fairly important	31
Not particularly important	14
Not important at all	8
Don't know	17

Six Americans in ten (61 percent) feel that continued U.S. support for the security of the people in Taiwan is either very or fairly important to them personally when they consider the question of recognizing the People's Republic.

This outlook is shared with little variation by most Americans. Republicans are most concerned about the security of Taiwan, 70 percent deeming it very or fairly important. Among Democrats, 57 percent agree, as do 61 percent of Independents.

The college-educated are also very concerned about Taiwan's security; 69 percent consider it very or fairly important. Those with grade school education have the least concern: only 42 percent consider Taiwan's security important. In this and most other cases, those with grade school educations record an unusually high number of "don't knows," reflecting lack of concern, lack of knowledge, or both.

For many Americans, however, concern for the security of the people of Taiwan is one thing, but specific U.S. action in their defense is something else. The responses to the final two questions in the 1977 survey demonstrate this:

> *Suppose the United States broke off diplomatic and defense treaty relations with the Republic of China, on Taiwan, and established full diplomatic relations with mainland China, on the assumption that mainland China would not use force against Taiwan. And suppose further that sometime later mainland China attacked Taiwan in order to take it over. Would you favor or oppose the U.S. coming directly to the defense of Taiwan with our naval and air forces?*

Favor	36%
Oppose	40
Don't know	24

If "opposed" or "don't know," ask:

> *In the event of such an attack, would you favor or oppose helping Taiwan defend itself by sending military supplies only, without involving our own armed forces?*

Favor	46%
Oppose	28
Don't know	26

In framing these questions, possible U.S. involvement was deliberately limited in the first instance to the use of naval and air forces, excluding ground troops. The response is essentially a standoff, with the glass half full or half empty, depending on one's point of view. The fact that 36 percent of the public are prepared in the abstract to defend Taiwan is impressive, particularly in light of the caution about foreign commitments that Americans are displaying in the aftermath of the Vietnam war. Furthermore, this level of support very easily might increase if mainland China did, in fact, attack Taiwan, depending on the closeness of our relations with Taiwan at the time, where the President positioned himself, and how he explained the stakes in terms of U.S. national interests.

On the other hand, the fact that a substantial majority (64 percent) are either opposed to this level of commitment or do not have an opinion is also impressive. And among this majority, less than half (46 percent) are prepared to come to the defense of Taiwan with military supplies only. What some would label a minimal level of support for an ally—aid in the form of supplies only—does not even command majority backing among those unwilling to endorse outright military intervention.

This reluctance to come to the defense of Taiwan is underscored by the more negative responses to a somewhat similar question in the 1978 survey. As discussed in chapter 1, 48 percent of Americans disagree with the proposition that "The United States should come to the defense of the Republic of China on Taiwan with military force if it is attacked by Communist China from the mainland"; 32 percent agree, and 20 percent say they don't know.

An Ambivalent Public

While it might be comforting, or at least intellectually satisfying, to be able to wrap up all these responses and outlooks in a single, neat formulation, this is not possible. China and the perplexing China issue pose a dilemma that leaves the American people ambivalent. The principal elements in that ambivalence can be summarized as follows.

(1) Americans remain far more positive in their attitudes toward the Republic of China on Taiwan than toward the People's Republic on the mainland.

(2) Americans view the expanding power and importance of the People's Republic with some anxiety, which contributes to an unwillingness to enhance Peking's military capabilities against Moscow in the enduring Sino-Soviet rift.

(3) Although full diplomatic relations between the United States and the People's Republic are endorsed in principle by a clear majority of Americans, that majority quickly become a minority in the face of Peking's demands that the United States sever diplomatic and military security relations with Taiwan.

(4) Continued support for Taiwan is an overriding component of the thinking of most Americans on the China issue, but that commitment is tempered when the question arises of helping Taiwan militarily against possible attack from the mainland. The consequences of the reality that the United States is caught up directly in a civil war, with the potential that carries for military involvement, are not easily digested by most Americans.

What all this seems to mean is that a settlement of the China issue, at least on terms acceptable to the majority of Americans, may require a set of compromises concerning the status and future of Taiwan beyond Peking's and Washington's willingness and ability thus far to negotiate. Creation of a stable triangle, one that adequately meets the basic interests of the parties concerned, presents an enormous challenge to policy makers and leaders in all three capitals.

Notes

1. See especially W. Watts and L. Free, *State of the Nation III* (Lexington, Mass.: Lexington Books, D.C. Heath, 1978), pp. 134-136.

9 A Look to the Future

In a more rational and orderly world, the issue of United States' relations with China—both the People's Republic and Taiwan—would have been resolved long since. But conflicting interests and claims continue to stand in the way and are likely to persist for some time.

To Normalize or Not?

The arguments for and against the United States moving ahead to establish full diplomatic relations with Peking have been set forth in the preceding pages; so, too, have various formulas for achieving this end. Any solution must be premised on the principle that the United States not act in a way that would destine Taiwan to forced annexation to the mainland. Both the United States and the People's Republic must consider a flexible position that facilitates normalization while recognizing and protecting the interests of the people of Taiwan.

Furthermore, both Washington and Peking must contemplate the possibility that failure in the quest for normalization could result not just in a continuation of the status quo, although that is certainly a possibility, and not an altogether undesirable one. But another possible outcome would be far more ominous—a gradual or even rapid deterioration in relations between the United States and the People's Republic. What path such a development might follow cannot be predicted, but the history of Sino-American relations is marked by wide swings from euphoria to enmity. There is no good reason to say this cannot happen again. Renewed enmity at a minimum would pose a direct threat to the stability of East and Northeast Asia. Such a prospect, however uncertain, cannot be tossed aside lightly.

Benefits of Normalization

If, however, normalization could be reached in the next couple of years, it would enhance the prospects for further improvement in relations between the United States and the People's Republic of China. Visits to the United States by high-level Chinese officials would become possible. American journalists could open offices in Peking, and Chinese journalists in Washington. Trade would probably increase somewhat, although economic constraints will prevent China for a long time from becoming an important trading partner of the United States. Ports and airports in the two countries would be opened to each other's ships and aircraft. Trade exhibits could be held in each country. Cultural exchanges and other travel between the United States and the People's Republic would become more consequential, although the differences in the two societies and political systems would continue to impose limits on the exchange process. In short, improvements in bilateral relations as a result of normalization would be modest but tangible.

A more important consequence of overcoming the obstacles to normalization would be to provide both nations with the confidence that now they were better able to pursue parallel policies based on common interests. For example, each would be in a stronger position to negotiate with the Soviet Union. The possibility of Sino-American agreement on arrangements to reduce the risk of war in Korea would be enhanced. The United States would be better able to use its influence to encourage the settlement of disputes between the People's Republic and countries nearby concerning undersea resources on the continental shelf. Conflict in Southeast Asia could be dealt with more readily.

Problems that Would Remain

The establishment of full diplomatic relations between the United States and the People's Republic would not, of course, ensure resolution of any of these difficult and complicated East Asian problems. Important differences between Washington and Peking would remain. Nevertheless, normalization of relations would improve in a general way the prospects for maintaining a peaceful, four-power equilibrium in East Asia.

Nor should it be assumed that a compromise on Taiwan reached in negotiating the normalization of U.S. relations with the People's Republic would "resolve" the Taiwan problem. Taiwan would continue to exist as a separate political entity with extensive relations with the United States, Japan, and many other countries. The People's Republic would be unlikely to abandon its objective of gaining control of Taiwan. On the contrary, the PRC, encouraged by its success in persuading the United States to curtail its official relations with Taiwan, might well redouble its efforts both to isolate the island and to convince its people that they have no choice but ultimate submission to the mainland's control. Forms of pressure available to Peking, short of military force, range from economic sanctions against foreign firms doing business with Taiwan to the threat of blockading the offshore islands or Taiwan itself.

Although the people of Taiwan would be disturbed by a U.S. compromise with mainland China, they would be unlikely to yield readily to pressure from the mainland. If the United States and Japan maintained their extensive economic relations with Taiwan, the island's economy would probably continue to grow rapidly, assuming a continued overall stability of the international economy, whose health affects Taiwan so directly. The personal ties with the mainland of those who came to Taiwan after World War II, already attenuated by a quarter of a century of separation, will erode rapidly as the older generation of mainlanders dies. The steady gain in influence on the government of the Republic of China of the 15 million native Taiwanese will further weaken the bond with the mainland.

Challenge and Opportunity

The United States will have to decide what policy will best serve its interests in the long term. As is true so often in international relations, choices at either end of the spectrum have, as discussed earlier, their particular dangers. Unconditional acceptance of Peking's conditions probably would spell disaster for Taiwan and would raise fundamental questions both here and abroad about the will and commitment of the United States. Doing nothing and attempting to preserve the status quo indefinitely runs the risk of a cooling of relations between the United States and the People's Republic, or worse.

The challenge to negotiators, and perhaps most of all to President Carter and his administration, is to define the intermediate avenue, the as yet unchartered path that can come closest to meeting the legitimate concerns of all involved. Both Americans and the Chinese must maintain allegiance to basic principles; and steps already taken by Washington and Peking, symbolized by the Nixon journey of 1972, show that compromise is possible. A middle road needs to be constructed in such a way as to avoid panic and disarray in Taiwan, perhaps best achieved by acceptance of a short-term adjustment concerning its status and leaving the long-term solution to the Chinese themselves. The policy path chartered must also reassure Japan and not undermine the shaky but nonetheless enduring truce in Korea.

All this is not necessarily an impossible task, but it would require an interrelated set of compromises that up to now the parties concerned have been unwilling to accept.

The United States can terminate its current formal diplomatic and military ties with Taiwan. But either the United States will want specific assurance from the People's Republic that the ultimate resolution of the status of Taiwan will be reached without resort to force, or else the United

States will need to create a new security arrangement with Taiwan that will protect the island's integrity and let it work out its own future links with the mainland through peaceful discussions. Given the level of compromise that cutting present ties with Taiwan would constitute, the United States would have good cause to insist that the People's Republic accept such reassurances for Taiwan.

To be sure, the People's Republic has indicated that it wants more, or at least that it is not prepared to compromise on "principles" related to Taiwan. But Peking has shown itself ready in the past to change course in pursuit of its larger objectives. In view of the scope of the bargaining and the magnitude of the U.S. undertaking involved, Peking may decide that its own interests do permit another step.

The fact remains that ultimately the Taiwan question is one for the Chinese themselves—on both sides of the straits—to resolve, a reality Americans do not contest. Taiwan, naturally, prefers the status quo, but would probably accommodate to the kind of arrangement set forth here. Its own freedom of choice would be protected.

The political risks inherent in any set of next steps in U.S. policy toward China are great. They are great not just for President Carter, but also for Chairman Hua and President Chiang. There are those in all three capitals, one can assume, who will press for more or less. Ultimately some degree of opposition will form against whatever set of actions is chosen.

Building a consensus and handling the inevitable opposition is what inspired political leadership is all about. Development of such a consensus in this country is not, our new survey suggests, beyond the reach of such leadership.

Public opinion in this country is neither fixed nor immutable. The American people are ready for a more complete relationship with the People's Republic of China, but within the framework of a decent respect for the rights of the people of Taiwan. Such broad guidelines give President Carter a considerable amount of territory within which to maneuver, to refine and even enlarge his options. The guidelines also suggest considerable need for public education and understanding. The China question remains a domestic as well as an international issue, with all the opportunities and pitfalls that implies.

Appendix
A Note on Survey
Research

The survey research which serves as the basis for the analysis in this book is the result of a national sampling of Americans conducted in two phases through the technical facilities of The Gallup Organization of Princeton, New Jersey. The authors, in consultation with Dr. Lloyd A. Free, president of the Institute for International Social Research, and Charles W. Roll, Jr., a noted authority in the field of public opinion, are responsible for the design and content of the questionnaire. The sampling procedure used in the fieldwork was designed by The Gallup Organization to produce an approximation of the total adult civilian population (eighteen years of age and older) living in the United States, except those persons in institutions such as prisons or hospitals. Demographic categories into which the sample was broken include sex, age, education, region of country, and politics. The authors analyzed and interpreted all of the data.

Fieldwork for the battery of questions on China, contained in part III, was carried out in April 1977, with personal interviews of 820 Americans. Fieldwork for parts I and II was carried out in April 1978, with a total of 1546 personal interviews conducted for those questions that cover both Japan and Korea. The survey ballot was split for questions applying solely to one country, with 770 individuals interviewed on Korea and 776 on Japan.

Index

Index

Africa: horn of, 103; Soviet expansion into, 109; and Third World States, 79

Agriculture and farm products: American, 56, 106-107, 109; Japanese, 54, 65

Aid: economic, 73, 92-93, 116-117; foreign, 75; military, 92-93; and South Korea, 92-94; Taiwan, 108, 116-117

Aircraft, types and supply of, 22, 117

Alaska, 25, 27; oil in, 24-25

Allies, U.S. defense of, 38-40

American Chamber of Commerce in Taipei, 117

"American formula," 121

American-Japanese alliance, 16

Anglo-Japanese alliance of 1902, 29

Anti-American nationalism in China, 111

Anti-Japanese trend, 32, 53

Antisubmarine warfare, 22

Archaeological exhibit in China, 107, 109

Armed forces: in Europe, 19; in Japan, 17, 49; occupational, 18, 41-43, 53, 81; Russian, 19; in South Korea, 20, 42, 64, 69, 95, 97; in Taiwan, 19, 107; in Thailand, 19; withdrawal of from South Korea, 4, 19, 36, 57, 64, 69, 81-85, 94-95, 99, 113

Armistice agreements, 66, 68, 79, 85, 97

Arms control, 114

Arms race, 83, 99

Arms sales, 22, 133

Asakai, Koichiro, 8

Asia: affairs of, 32-33, 40-41, 104-105; Chinese communist power in, 116; East, 14, 18-19, 81, 110, 113, 140; nationalism in, 8; oil-rich areas of, 113; Russian power in, 16, 19, 21, 109; South, 109; Southeast, 13-16, 79, 109, 140

Association of Southeast Asian Nations, 15

Atomic bomb, 4

Australia, 116

Authoritarian political systems, 64, 74, 81

Automakers, 29

Balance-of-payments, problems of, 7, 25-27, 31

Banking interests, 10

Barnwell, South Carolina, 24

Bases, military and naval, 17, 20, 22, 53

Big Powers and Korea, 64-69

Bilateral diplomatic relations, 79, 92, 97, 105, 111-112, 115, 140

Blockades and threats of, 113, 118, 140

Boeing Company, 57, 107

Bonin Islands, 6, 16

Brazil, 34-35

Breeder reactors, 24, 57

Bribery scandals, 9, 71

Brzezinski, Zbigniew, 103, 108

"Buy American" sentiment, 51

Cairo Declaration, 65, 115

California, 27

Cambodia, 16

Canada, 25, 34, 126

Cartels (zaibatsu), huge, 4

Carter, Chip, 103

Carter, James Earl: administration of, 4, 19-20, 64, 69, 94-95, 119-120, 123, 131, 136, 142; foreign policy advisers, 31, 103; middle-of-the-road policies, 79-80, 83; and plutonium, 23; Sino-American relations, 108-109; on Taiwan, 121, 134; troop withdrawal policy, 4, 19, 36, 57, 64, 69, 81-85, 94-95, 99, 113

Central Intelligence Agency (CIA): Korea, 63, 72; United States, 74

Chai Tse-min, diplomat, 103

About the Authors

William Watts, president of Potomac Associates, is coauthor of several Potomac publications. He served in the U.S. Foreign Service in Moscow and Seoul, and in the Office of Asian Communist Affairs in the State Department. Prior to founding Potomac Associates, he served as a program officer in the Office of Policy and Planning at the Ford Foundation, was a director of the New York State Office for Urban Innovation, and worked for The National Security Council in the White House.

George R. Packard is deputy director of the Woodrow Wilson International Center for Scholars at the Smithsonian Institution in Washington, D.C. He served as special assistant to Ambassador Edwin O. Reischauer in the American Embassy in Tokyo, 1963-65, and was diplomatic correspondent for *Newsweek* magazine and executive editor of the *Philadelphia Bulletin* after that. He is author of *Protest in Tokyo,* which deals with the political turmoil over the U.S.-Japan Security Treaty of 1960, attended Tokyo University, and has resided in Japan for more than six years.

Ralph N. Clough is a former foreign service officer who spent thirteen years in mainland China, Hong Kong, and Taiwan. He was a director of the Office of Chinese Affairs in the State Department and a member of the Policy Planning Council. He is the author of *East Asia and U.S. Security, Deterrence and Defense in Korea: The Role of U.S. Forces,* and *Island China.* He has received fellowships at the Brookings Institution and the Woodrow Wilson International Center for Scholars, where he is currently located.

Robert B. Oxnam, formerly associate professor of history at Trinity College, is program director of the China Council of The Asia Society. The China Council is a national public education center on Chinese affairs. Dr. Oxnam's recent publications include: coauthor with Michel Oksenberg, *China and America: Past and Future,* and coeditor with Michel Oksenberg, *Dragon and Eagle: Sino-American Relations in Historical Perspective.* He has visited both Taiwan and the People's Republic of China.